PREPARED TO PREVAIL

A complete guide to living ready in an uncertain world

Trevor DeGroote

Copyright © 2025 by Trevor DeGroote
All rights reserved.

No part of this publication may be reproduced, distributed, or transmitted in any form or by any means, including photocopying, recording, or other electronic or mechanical methods, without the prior written permission of the publisher, except in the case of brief quotations embodied in critical reviews and certain other noncommercial uses permitted by copyright law.

For permission requests, write to the publisher at: preparedtoprevail.com

First Edition, 2025

Printed in the United States of America.

The information in this book is intended for educational purposes only. The author and publisher assume no responsibility or liability for any injuries, damages, or losses that may occur as a result of applying the information contained herein. Readers are encouraged to use discretion and seek legal guidance when appropriate.

CONTENTS

Introduction 1

Chapter 1: The Defender's Mind 3

Chapter 2: Living Awake 11

Chapter 3: Built To Endure 21

Chapter 4: The Anatomy of Awareness 30

Chapter 5: Principles of Defensive Action 40

Chapter 6: Tools With Purpose 48

Chapter 7: The Stronghold: Home and Vehicle Preparedness 57

Chapter 8: Strategy of Survival 69

Chapter 9: The Aftermath 80

Chapter 10: The Defender's Discipline 89

Chapter 11: Enduring Readiness 98

Conclusion: A Life Prepared to Prevail 104

INTRODUCTION

Life has always carried within it a tension between beauty and danger. One moment we are surrounded by peace, routine, and ordinary joys, and the next we may find ourselves confronted with a crisis. No one chooses the moment when adversity arrives. No one schedules the instant when fear presses close, when safety is threatened, or when responsibility can no longer be delayed. Still, whether we acknowledge it or not, those moments will come, and when they do, the only valid variable is whether we are ready to meet them.

Preparedness is not about living in fear or expecting harm at every turn. It is about living awake, choosing to see the world as it is, rather than as we wish it to be, and preparing ourselves accordingly. To prepare is to love life enough to defend it. It is to accept that peace is not maintained through wishful thinking but through vigilance, clarity, and strength anchored in principle. Those who prepare are not seeking conflict; they are cultivating the ability to stand firm when conflict finds them. Their readiness is not born of paranoia, but of compassion; for their families, for their communities, and for the lives entrusted to their care.

This book is written for those who refuse to be passive participants in their own story. Within these chapters, you will find not just tactics or tools but the deeper foundations of a defender's life: the philosophy and mentality that give purpose to preparation, the awareness that sharpens perception, the conditioning that strengthens both body and mind, the judgment that discerns risk, the discipline that defuses conflict, and the wisdom to employ tools responsibly. Each element builds upon the others, forming a comprehensive framework that equips ordinary people to prevail in extraordinary circumstances.

The path of preparedness is not a temporary project but a way of life. It asks us to cultivate habits of awareness and discipline, to strengthen both character and skill, and to anchor every choice in the conviction that life is worth protecting. This is not a burden, but a freedom. It is the freedom to live with confidence rather than anxiety, to move through the world with eyes open and heart steady, knowing that while we cannot control what storms may come, we can decide who we will be when they arrive.

The pages that follow are an invitation to embrace this way of living, not with fear, but with courage; not with suspicion, but with clarity; not with aggression, but with love. To live prepared is to accept both the fragility and the value of life, and to take responsibility for safeguarding it. In doing so, we declare that fear will not rule us, that chaos will not define us, and that when the moment of testing comes, we will be ready to stand, to protect, and to prevail.

CHAPTER 1

THE DEFENDER'S MIND

Human beings are creatures of both fragility and potential. We are capable of immense compassion and creation, yet we exist within a world that can be unpredictable, indifferent, and at times cruel. It is this paradox, the coexistence of beauty and danger, that compels thoughtful individuals to live prepared. To live prepared is not to expect harm or to walk through life with suspicion; it is to accept reality as it is and to take responsibility for our role within it. The decision to prepare oneself to protect life, our own and that of others, is an act rooted not in fear, but in love. It arises from a recognition that life is precious, fleeting, and deserving of preservation. This philosophy underpins a life lived in readiness: the philosophy of the loving defender.

The loving defender does not seek conflict, but understands that peace cannot be sustained by wishful thinking alone. They recognize that safety is not a guarantee granted by others, but a condition that must be maintained through awareness, competence, and moral clarity. The mindset of preparedness begins when an individual refuses to live as a passive participant in their own story. It starts when one acknowledges that there will be moments in life, rare, unpredictable, and often uninvited, when the ability to act decisively can mean the difference between tragedy and survival. Preparedness is not merely an accumulation of skills or equipment; it is the steady cultivation of character.

A life of readiness begins with humility. To prepare oneself is to admit vulnerability, to recognize that evil, chaos, and danger exist in the world, and that none of us is immune. Many people avoid this acknowledgment because it is uncomfortable; they prefer the illusion that bad things happen only to others. However, denial is not peace; it is elected blindness disguised as comfort. The loving defender faces reality with courage, not cynicism. They see the world as it truly is, both the good and the bad, and they choose to stand as a protector within it. This humility breeds wisdom. It acknowledges that safety cannot be outsourced, that law enforcement and emergency services, while invaluable, cannot be everywhere at once. Actual preparedness begins where dependency ends.

To live prepared is to take ownership of one's sphere of influence. It means understanding that the first line of protection for any person, family, or community is not an institution; it is the individual who chooses to be ready. This sense of personal responsibility transforms ordinary people into guardians, not out of a desire for control, but out of a sense of service. It is an act of stewardship, an acknowledgment that those who can prepare have a moral duty to do so. A parent does not prepare because they expect danger at every corner; they prepare because they love their child enough to refuse helplessness. A citizen does not learn to act under stress because they crave confrontation; they do so because they wish to live free and unafraid, capable of responding to a crisis rather than collapsing beneath it.

At the heart of this philosophy lies a reverence for life itself. The defender's purpose is not destruction but preservation.

Violence, when it must be confronted, is met not with malice but with restraint, purpose, and the clear intent to end harm as swiftly as possible. The prepared individual understands that force, when used righteously, is an extension of mercy. It stops evil from advancing, not to punish, but to protect. This moral clarity separates the defender from the aggressor. The aggressor acts from ego, dominance, or hatred; the defender acts from love, duty, and necessity. This difference in motivation is what grants peace even in the midst of chaos.

Preparedness is also a philosophy of discipline. The loving defender knows that readiness cannot be faked or improvised in the moment of need. It must be cultivated daily through consistent choices, habits, and a deliberate mindset. Discipline is expressed not only through training but through restraint, patience, and judgment. To live prepared means to maintain awareness without paranoia, confidence without arrogance, and vigilance without hostility. It means to control oneself before attempting to prevent any circumstance. The untrained person may react out of panic or pride; the disciplined individual responds with calm precision because they have already rehearsed what others never imagine.

Adopting this lifestyle requires a transformation of how one sees the world. It is not enough to carry tools or attend classes; one must have a purpose. Preparedness becomes a lens through which all decisions are filtered. It influences where we go, how we move, who we trust, and what risks we accept. It encourages simplicity, fewer distractions, and fewer vulnerabilities, replacing complacency with intentionality. The prepared individual does not drift through life on autopilot. Every action is deliberate, and every environment is assessed, not out of anxiety, but out of awareness. Awareness is love in motion, the act of caring enough to pay attention.

Central to this philosophy is the understanding that preparedness is not a selfish act; rather, it is a responsible and prudent approach. It is not just about personal survival, but also about contributing to the safety and strength of others. The loving defender understands that when each person accepts responsibility for their own readiness, the entire community benefits. Safety multiplies through example. When one person chooses to learn medical skills, another is saved in an emergency. When one person maintains situational awareness, they warn others before danger spreads. Preparedness ripples outward, shaping a culture of responsibility where apathy once reigned. The defender does not hoard capability; they share it, teach it, and model it. Their life becomes a quiet form of leadership.

The mindset of preparedness is not fueled by hatred or distrust; it is grounded in a spirit of peace. Peace, however, is not merely the absence of conflict. It is characterized by stability, confidence, and readiness. True peace is maintained through strength, and strength without moral direction becomes tyranny. Therefore, the loving defender anchors their strength in compassion. They do not train to dominate others, but to serve them. They do not prepare because they expect violence, but because they reject victimhood. To live prepared is to say, "I will not let fear dictate my choices, nor will I let evil have the final word."

Living prepared also means understanding human nature. Conflict, danger, and disorder are not new; they are constants in the story of humanity. What changes is how we respond to them. Civilization itself depends on people who are willing to stand between chaos and the innocent, who choose courage over complacency. It does not require everyone to be a warrior, but it does require a warrior's heart: a heart disciplined by love, guided by principle, and unwilling to abdicate responsibility. A society built entirely on dependence quickly crumbles when systems fail. A society of prepared, capable, compassionate individuals endures.

Psychologically, preparedness reshapes the individual. It creates a shift from helplessness to control. Many people go through life believing that fate, luck, or the government will decide their outcomes. The prepared person rejects this passivity. They accept uncertainty but refuse to surrender to it. Preparedness teaches that fear can be managed, chaos can be organized, and crisis can be survived through intention and training. It builds confidence, which in turn breeds calm. The person who knows what to do under pressure radiates stability; they become an anchor for those around them.

Yet the philosophy of preparedness also demands humility in strength. Competence without character is dangerous. The loving defender must always pair capability with conscience. This means constantly examining motives, ensuring that the desire for readiness never devolves into ego or a sense of superiority. The goal is not to feel powerful, but to be responsible. The defender does not seek validation through confrontation; they seek fulfillment through service. Every tool, every skill, every plan exists not to inflate pride, but to protect life.

Ethical grounding is therefore essential. To prepare to defend is to prepare to make moral decisions under duress. The moment of crisis will not allow for philosophical debate; it will demand immediate judgment. That judgment must be pre-anchored in principles: proportionality, necessity, and the sanctity of life. The loving defender rehearses not only actions, but intentions. They know where their moral line lies, and they have resolved, long before the moment comes, what they will and will not do. This moral preparation ensures that when action is required, it is taken with clarity and righteousness rather than confusion or regret.

Preparedness is also an act of stewardship toward one's own body and mind. The body is the vessel through which all actions flow. Neglect of health, fitness, or mental discipline weakens one's ability to respond effectively when needed. The prepared life, therefore, values wellness, balance, and continual growth. It views training not as punishment, but as a gesture of gratitude and the acknowledgment that the body's strength is a gift to be nurtured and maintained. Mental training is equally vital. Composure, emotional regulation, and awareness must be practiced until they become second nature. The defender who cannot control their emotions becomes their own liability. Thus, mastery of the self is the first step toward mastery of defense.

Living prepared does not mean living afraid. In fact, those who are most ready are often the most peaceful. Fear thrives in ignorance and uncertainty; confidence grows through competence. The person who knows they can act does not panic when danger appears. Instead, they meet it with measured calm. Preparedness replaces anxiety with assurance, replacing the question "What if?" with the answer "I am ready." It transforms fear into focus and transforms weakness into responsibility.

One of the most profound aspects of the loving defender's mindset is the rejection of apathy. Indifference to suffering, danger, or injustice is a quiet form of decay. The prepared individual refuses to look away when something is wrong. They act, not out of aggression, but out of a sense of duty. Whether it is intervening to stop harm, offering aid after an accident, or simply educating others, the defender understands that inaction is a decision too. To live ready is to choose to be part of the solution rather than a spectator to tragedy.

At the same time, the defender's mindset is guided by discernment. Not every situation requires intervention; not every challenge is theirs to solve. Wisdom lies in knowing when to act and when to withdraw. This balance between courage and caution is refined through experience, reflection, and a humble approach. The defender studies not only tactics but human behavior, law, and psychology, recognizing that the best way to protect life is often through prevention and de-escalation. The highest victory is not in defeating an attacker, but in preventing the attack altogether.

Preparedness is a long-term commitment, not a temporary project. It must evolve with the individual. As seasons of life change, so too must our preparation methods. A college student's readiness differs from that of a parent, a retiree, or a traveler abroad. However, the principles remain constant: awareness, responsibility, and love. These are the pillars that sustain the lifestyle. To live prepared is to cultivate habits that promote safety without compromising joy. It is not about living smaller, but about living wiser.

Ultimately, the philosophy of preparedness is an expression of hope. It declares that life is worth defending, that good is worth preserving, and that ordinary people can rise to extraordinary moments through intentional living. It invites each of us to adopt a posture of service rather than submission, and to cultivate courage rather than complacency. Preparedness does not seek to dominate the world; it aims to preserve the beauty within it.

When we live prepared, we send a message to those around us: that fear will not rule, that chaos will not dictate, and that love, disciplined, grounded, and courageous, will always take its rightful place as the foundation of strength. The loving defender stands not on the edge of paranoia, but at the intersection of awareness and compassion. They are steady, humble, and ready. Their preparation is not a burden, but a form of peace.

To live prepared is to live awake, to walk through life, eyes open, heart steady, and purpose clear. It is to accept that we cannot predict the storms that may come, but we can decide the kind of person we will be when they arrive. And when that moment comes, whether it is a split-second crisis or a lifetime of challenges, the loving defender will already have made their choice: to protect life, to serve others, and to prevail not through fear, but through readiness grounded in love.

CHAPTER 2

LIVING AWAKE

The downtown streets had quieted for the evening, the once-busy sidewalks now lightly traveled. The buzz of office workers and delivery trucks had faded into a distant hum of occasional passing cars, and most of the tall office buildings had gone dark, their rows of windows reflecting only the faint glow of streetlamps. Jessica stepped out of her building, adjusting the strap of her purse as the heavy glass door shut behind her. The breezy night air wafted over her skin, and she exhaled, wishing she had left earlier with the rest of her coworkers. Staying late to finish reports had seemed responsible at the time, but as she looked around at the empty street, she found herself regretting the decision. She wasn't afraid, at least not yet, but something about the stillness carried weight. Though she had walked this route many times before, a subtle unease told her tonight would be different.

At the top of the steps, she paused, taking a deliberate moment to study her surroundings before committing to the street. To most eyes, nothing seemed unusual, but Jessica noticed a man across the way leaning against a brick wall. He appeared to be in his late thirties, with a thin frame, and wore a thick jacket despite the sweat-inducing heat, even in the presence of a breeze. In one hand, he loosely held a cigarette, though no smoke rose from it, and in the other hand, a lighter flicked without ever igniting. He wasn't talking on the phone. He wasn't checking for a ride. He wasn't passing the time with any discernible purpose. He was just there, watching.

Jessica's instincts stirred. She didn't make a dramatic move, but she adjusted her route, crossing the street sooner than she usually would, putting space between herself and the man. Her stride remained steady, her posture casual, but her eyes worked like a camera lens, gathering details and storing them. As she rounded the next corner, another irregularity caught her attention: a vehicle idling at the entrance of an alley. The engine was on, but its headlights were dark. The tint on the windows was so deep she couldn't make out who, if anyone, was inside. Its position felt calculated, its presence unusual.

Trusting her gut, she slowed her stride as though she had reached her destination and turned smoothly into a corner coffee shop. Inside, the barista greeted her warmly, and Jessica ordered a drink, choosing a table near the front window. From that seat, she had a clear view of the sidewalk and the alley. Her demeanor remained calm, but her mind was alert, scanning for what would happen next.

Not long after, the man she had first noticed walked past the shop. He didn't hurry, but he paused briefly at the door, peering inside. His eyes swept the room in a searching way before he continued down the street. Jessica's pulse quickened, but she remained composed. She set her coffee aside, pulled out her phone, and called the non-emergency line at the police department. Her voice was steady and precise as she explained what she had seen: the man's behavior, the idle vehicle, the location, the timing. She reported without exaggeration, calmly and deliberately.

Minutes later, Jessica watched as the vehicle backed out of the alley, only to find itself caught between two patrol cars approaching from opposite directions. Officers stepped out and began speaking with the driver. By trusting her instincts, altering her behavior, and reporting what she saw, Jessica had disrupted what could have been a dangerous encounter.

The following morning, she received a call from a detective. He explained that the two men, the one who had lingered against the wall and the one waiting in the vehicle, were suspects in a series of muggings targeting women walking alone at night. Their method was deliberate: identify a lone target, communicate with each other, and stage an ambush near secluded areas. Jessica's decision to change her route, take shelter in a public space, and notify authorities had interfered with their plan. She hadn't run. She hadn't escalated. She hadn't needed to fight. She had simply observed, adjusted, and acted with presence of mind.

This story underscores one of the most fundamental principles of personal safety: situational awareness. Weapons, martial arts, and emergency responses are valuable, but none of them matter if you are caught entirely off guard. The first and most powerful tool you possess in self-defense is not what you carry in your hands but how you use your mind. Situational awareness is the discipline of perceiving, interpreting, and responding to your environment before a threat can fully materialize. It is the art of staying present in the world rather than drifting through it on autopilot. While most people associate danger with sudden force, the reality is that most victims are defeated first by surprise. When you eliminate surprise, you deny predators their greatest advantage.

Situational awareness begins with perception, and perception is more than merely seeing. It is the active process of noticing.

Cultivate the ability to detect subtle cues others overlook, the stranger who seems out of place near an entrance, the vehicle that does not fit the setting, the sudden silence in a group that had been speaking comfortably a moment before. These anomalies often pass unnoticed by those absorbed in routine, yet they are the very signals that can reveal danger. Perception is a learned discipline, honed through mindfulness and consistent practice. To be aware is not to live in paranoia, but to live awake and present in your surroundings, no matter where you are.

A structured framework for understanding decision-making through awareness is found in the OODA loop, developed by U.S. Air Force Colonel John Boyd. OODA stands for Observe, Orient, Decide, and Act, and it describes the continuous cycle through which all human beings process information and respond to circumstances. In a defensive context, mastering this cycle can mean the difference between safety and victimization. Observation is the intake of raw data. Orientation is the process of filtering and interpreting that information through the lens of your experience and environment. A decision is the moment of choosing a course of action. Action is the execution of that choice. The loop never ends; once you act, you are again observing the result, reorienting, deciding, and acting in a constant rhythm. Those who move fluidly through this cycle gain the ability to act quickly and decisively, while those who hesitate or skip steps find themselves behind the curve.

Observation, the first stage, is often underestimated. Many assume that they are "aware" because they are looking around, but true observation is an active process. It involves not only noting who and what is around you, but also how those elements fit or fail to fit into the setting. It is not about memorizing every detail but identifying the things that do not belong, like finding the twos in a sea of ones and zeroes. You scan doorways, hallways, and corners. You identify exits. You take note of lighting, of shadows, of crowd dynamics. You ask yourself quietly, 'Are people relaxed or tense? Who is paying attention to me, and who is lost in their own world? Who is watching the watchers?' By making observation a constant habit, you gradually train yourself to see what most people miss.

Orientation is the deeper layer, where information takes on meaning. It is shaped by your background, your training, and your experiences. Two people can see the same situation and interpret it differently depending on what they have learned. Someone familiar with criminal behavior might notice pre-assault cues that another dismisses as nerves. Orientation allows you to evaluate significance: is that hand in the pocket casual or concealing? Does that posture suggest relaxation or aggression? The more you study human behavior, the better you become at interpreting it. Orientation can be sharpened through scenario-based training, analyzing real incidents, and consciously reflecting on what is observed. It is here that you establish baselines for what is normal, which allows you to recognize what is not.

Decision is where clarity meets urgency. You cannot delay indefinitely. Time is a resource you never fully control, and in a confrontation, hesitation often carries a greater cost than making an imperfect choice. Decisions must be proportional to the threat but made without second-guessing. It may mean merely changing your route, leaving a particular environment, or preparing a defensive tool. The key is that the decision is made consciously, deliberately, and promptly. Mental rehearsal helps tremendously. By imagining scenarios such as what you would do if this person approached, if that door were blocked, or if this vehicle followed you, you build pathways in your mind that allow you to decide quickly when reality unfolds.

Action is where preparation becomes reality. Once you decide, you must execute with full commitment. If you leave, you leave. If you engage, you engage decisively. Half-measures invite confusion and embolden aggressors. Action grounded in careful observation, informed orientation, and clear decision-making often feels instinctual, but instinct is rarely natural; it is the result of repeated practice and preparation.

The practice of situational awareness extends beyond immediate threats and applies to the environments we move through every day. Consider transitional zones, those places where our context shifts quickly, such as parking garages, building entrances, or stairwells. These are moments when we are often distracted, preoccupied with entering or leaving, yet predators exploit them precisely because they create opportunity. Each time you transition environments, you must reset your awareness. Exiting a well-lit building into a dark street is not the same as walking down that street at noon. Lighting, exits, and visibility have changed, and so must your perception. You reestablish your scan: where are the cars, who is nearby, what paths are clear? Each recalibration reinforces your readiness.

Distraction is the enemy of awareness, and modern technology provides endless temptation. People walk with their eyes locked on their phones, ears sealed with earbuds, attention consumed by digital worlds, while the physical world moves on without them. This behavior creates perfect conditions for predators. Someone absorbed in their screen will not notice being followed, will not hear footsteps behind them, and will not register a vehicle slowing nearby. Situational awareness requires the discipline to disconnect in vulnerable environments. Your phone should not compete with your safety.

Equally dangerous is complacency. Familiarity breeds comfort, and comfort blinds. Many crimes occur not in strange, foreign places but in the very spaces people consider safe, their own driveways, workplaces, or neighborhoods. Offenders rely on the fact that when you feel at home, you let your guard down. Effective awareness means resisting that urge. Safety is not guaranteed simply because a place feels familiar. Vigilance in the ordinary is as essential as vigilance in the extraordinary.

The ability to recognize patterns is another essential element. Human beings are wired to see patterns, and in self-defense, this ability can expose threats. The car circling your block repeatedly, the individual whose pace matches yours step for step, the argument in the distance escalating in tone, these are patterns worth noting. By tuning yourself to deviations from the norm, you can identify risk long before it reaches you.

Body language is perhaps the most telling of all signals. Much of communication is nonverbal, and those preparing for aggression often telegraph their intentions with physical cues. Nervous fidgeting, glances at exits, concealed hands, clenched fists, shifting weight, all of these can precede action. By learning to interpret these signals, you can spot aggression forming before it erupts.

To help conceptualize awareness levels, Lt. Col. Jeff Cooper's color code system remains a valuable tool for understanding the concept.

Condition White is unawareness, a state of being distracted or complacent.

Condition Yellow is a relaxed alert state, the ideal state of calm vigilance for daily life.

Condition Orange is a heightened alert due to a specific anomaly or potential threat.

Condition Red is imminent action, the moment when a threat has materialized, and a response is required.

The goal is to live in Yellow, transitioning to Orange or Red as circumstances demand. This is not paranoia, but rather practiced attentiveness, a calm readiness that allows you to respond effectively.

Incorporating situational awareness into daily routines does not create fear; it builds confidence. The person who knows they are aware is less anxious, more secure, and better equipped to navigate uncertainty. Choosing where to sit in a restaurant, noting who enters and exits, and identifying emergency exits are simple habits that add layers of preparedness. With repetition, they stop feeling like an effort and begin to feel like a natural part of living.

Awareness is not just individual; it extends to groups, especially families. Teaching children to be observant, trust their instincts, and voice concerns builds collective safety. Everyday outings become opportunities to practice asking what they've noticed, discussing where exits are, and creating plans for separation. Families who cultivate awareness together are less likely to be isolated or taken by surprise.

For those who carry defensive tools, particularly firearms, awareness takes on even greater importance. A firearm introduces both capability and responsibility. You must be acutely aware not only of threats but also of bystanders, backgrounds, and environments. It is not enough to recognize danger; you must also ensure that your response does not create unintended harm. Responsible armed defense requires judgment as much as skill, and judgment begins with awareness.

Mental exercises are an effective way to strengthen awareness. Imagine scenarios as you move through life. What if someone entered this store aggressively? Where are the exits in this theater? How would I respond if I were followed in this parking garage? These quiet mental rehearsals prepare the mind to act decisively when reality demands it. The body resists going where the mind has never been.

Even at home, awareness plays a role. Your home is both a sanctuary and a potential target. Understanding vulnerabilities such as unlocked doors, poorly lit yards, and predictable routines allows you to reduce risk. Awareness of deliveries, vehicles, and neighborhood activity provides a more comprehensive picture of your environment. Security begins with recognition, and recognition comes from observation.

Neighborhood awareness is the extension of this principle. Communities that are observant, connected, and communicative are less attractive to criminals. Knowing your neighbors, watching for unusual activity, and sharing information are simple yet effective actions that foster a sense of collective safety. Isolation leaves individuals vulnerable; collaboration, on the other hand, strengthens everyone.

Ultimately, situational awareness is not a sole tactic but a mindset. It is the deliberate choice to remain present, to refuse complacency, and to cultivate perception. It is the recognition that safety is not about living in fear but about living with purpose, attentiveness, and readiness. The person who practices awareness consistently gains an advantage over those who drift blindly through their environment. They notice what others miss. They act before others react. They remain composed when others panic. Situational awareness is not paranoia; it is the practice of being alive to the world and prepared for whatever it may bring.

CHAPTER 3

BUILT TO ENDURE

Mike didn't expect anything out of the ordinary that Friday night. After all, it was just another late shift at the hospital, followed by a stop at the twenty-four-hour grocery store. He wasn't in uniform anymore; he had changed into a hoodie and joggers before leaving the staff locker room. The hospital's emergency department had been brutal that evening, with multiple trauma cases arriving back-to-back, a psychiatric patient suffering a meltdown, and even a brief power flicker that sent every machine into temporary chaos. Mike was exhausted, his body heavy with fatigue, but his composure remained intact. That composure was no accident. He had worked for years to build it, through morning workouts before long shifts, interval runs on his days off, and steady weight training three or four times a week. He didn't train for appearance or vanity; he trained because he remembered what it felt like to freeze. Three years earlier, he had been robbed at knife point, paralyzed and unable to move, breath shallow, mind blank. That moment had cut deeper than the threat itself, leaving behind a scar of vulnerability that transformed into a vow. From that night forward, he had sworn never again to hand total control to a predator.

That promise had driven him to immerse himself in both physical training and mental conditioning. He had joined a local gym that specialized in Muay Thai and Brazilian Jiu-Jitsu, pouring himself into drills that taught his body to move fluidly and decisively under pressure. He practiced box breathing during quiet breaks at work, forcing his heart rate under control while alarms blared in the distance. He studied books on high-stress decision-making, joined friends in force-on-force scenarios with airsoft guns, obtained his concealed carry permit, and competed in monthly pistol matches to keep his skills sharp. He never fantasized about using those skills; he simply refused to leave his survival entirely in someone else's hands.

Now, walking behind the dimly lit grocery store with plastic bags swinging at his side, the late summer air clinging to his skin, Mike felt the soreness of that morning's deadlifts in his legs. He welcomed the ache because it reminded him of his preparation. However, as he approached his truck at the far end of the lot, the hairs on his neck rose. A faint sound in the silence pricked his senses, a subtle shuffling that confirmed he was not alone. He slowed, scanning instinctively left and right before lowering his bags to the pavement, freeing his hands.

From between two parked cars five spots down, a man emerged. Young, athletic, hoodie drawn low, hands not visible, his posture radiating intent. He was not walking toward the store or a vehicle; he was angling directly toward Mike. Mike's heart rate surged, but his breathing stayed steady as he drew a deliberate breath. He had felt adrenaline before, in the chaos of resuscitating a crashing patient, in sparring matches, in staged confrontations where every mistake was punished. He knew how panic could creep in, but he also learned how to climb above it.

The man spoke casually, "You got the time?" Mike did not answer. He stepped back, eyes fixed on the man's hands. That's when he caught the glint of steel: a folding knife held low, partially hidden behind a thigh. Mike did not freeze. He did not wait. He moved. Years of Muay Thai footwork surged alive in his legs as he sidestepped behind the cover of a sedan, putting metal between them. His right hand dipped under his hoodie where his concealed pistol rested, but he did not draw. Not yet. His voice rang out sharp and firm, "Stay back! Walk away."

The man faltered at the unexpected confidence. The routine had been disrupted. The blade dipped slightly, but then the attacker slowly nudged forward, closing the gap. Mike pivoted smoothly, drawing now, pistol up, balanced, controlled. His voice cracked through the night: "Stop! Drop the knife!" His stance, his breath, his eyes, all radiated preparation, not fear. This move wasn't bravado. It was readiness. Then, the man froze, hesitating, as his instincts screamed that this would not go as planned. He turned and ran.

Mike did not chase. He backed away cautiously, eyes scanning, pistol still low and ready until he reached the shelter of his truck. Only then did he holster carefully and call 911. Minutes later, police arrived, and store cameras confirmed the encounter. The attacker was arrested nearby while attempting to break into a vehicle, with the same knife and the same hoodie. When Mike gave his statement, he spoke with clarity, detailing every step and every decision with restraint. Officers noted his composure. Later, alone in his truck, Mike finally felt the tremor of adrenaline leave his body. His hands shook briefly. He closed his eyes and steadied his breath, inhale, hold, exhale, count by four. Relief replaced fear. He did not feel powerful, nor victorious, only thankful. Years of preparation had delivered him home safely. He had not crossed the line; he had stood firmly on the line he had drawn for himself.

This story illustrates the essence of physical conditioning and mental preparedness, which are not optional extras in self-defense but foundational pillars. A strong, trained body and a resilient, disciplined mind form the twin engines that power survival in high-stress encounters. A person who builds physical capability without mental resilience risks panic when the moment demands clarity, while someone who hones their mindset without physical capacity risks collapse when the body cannot perform. Survival capability and effective defensive action emerge from the union of both. Physical training empowers the body to endure, resist, and act. Mental training equips the mind to direct those actions with composure, discipline, and legality. Together, they create not just the possibility but the probability of prevailing.

Physical conditioning begins with the most elemental components of human performance: cardiovascular endurance, muscular strength, stamina, flexibility, and mobility. Cardio fitness enhances the body's capacity to move continuously, escape, or fight without immediate exhaustion. A defender with trained lungs and a strong heart can sprint across a parking lot, wrestle free of an attacker, or endure minutes of struggle without collapsing. Strength training provides the raw capacity to push, pull, grip, and resist, which in real encounters may be the difference between breaking free or being overpowered. Flexibility and mobility reduce the risk of injury and expand the range of motion, allowing for fluid strikes, evasive turns, or quick recoveries from awkward positions. Every aspect of fitness directly contributes to the ability to act decisively in defense.

For many people, fitness is often framed in terms of appearance; however, in the context of self-defense, it is viewed as a matter of survival. Being able to climb stairs without gasping, run a mile, or carry one's own body weight translates into practical competence. Foundational bodyweight exercises such as squats, push-ups, planks, burpees, and pull-ups deliver resilience that underpins any martial art or defensive tactic. High-intensity cardio routines, such as interval sprints, swimming laps, or jump rope drills, mimic the bursts of exertion typical of intense physical activity. Balance and coordination drills refine the small but vital margins that determine whether one stays standing or is driven to the ground. None of these is needed to create a professional athlete; they simply create a human being capable of responding under duress.

The next level of conditioning often comes through structured martial arts or combat sports. Disciplines like Brazilian Jiu-Jitsu, Boxing, Muay Thai, Wrestling, Judo, or Krav Maga not only improve physical attributes but also teach timing, distance, leverage, and composure in the presence of resistance. Sparring against resisting opponents inoculates the body and mind against shock, replacing panic with practiced responses. Through these systems, the body learns efficient movement while the mind learns humility, patience, and confidence. The goal is not to train for trophies or belts, but for survival, giving one the ability to respond fluidly when an attack is sudden and chaotic.

Equally crucial is mental preparedness, the companion to physical ability. The mind governs the choices made when seconds decide outcomes. A prepared mind recognizes the surge of adrenaline not as a cause for panic but as fuel for focused action. The fight-flight-freeze response is natural, but training reprograms its pathways, teaching the individual to act with purpose rather than succumb to paralysis. This training begins with visualization, a practice that involves mentally rehearsing scenarios to prepare for them. By imagining the sudden appearance of an assailant, the sound of breaking glass, or the escalation of an argument, the mind builds neural patterns that reduce hesitation. When reality presents similar cues, the brain recognizes the script and triggers prepared actions.

Beyond visualization lies stress inoculation. This is the deliberate practice of exposing oneself to pressure and unpredictability in controlled settings. Sparring while fatigued, drilling under time constraints, and running sprints before practicing fine motor skills all train the mind to stay sharp under duress. The objective is not to eliminate discomfort but to become comfortable within it, so that discomfort no longer rules behavior. Stress inoculation inhibits responses such as tunnel vision, preserves breathing rhythm, and sharpens decision-making when adrenaline surges.

A key element of mental preparedness is cultivating a resilient mindset. Resilience means the determination not to give in to fear, injury, or chaos. It does not glorify violence but accepts its possibility and refuses hesitation when violence becomes unavoidable. This mindset is built on clarity of purpose: deciding in advance what you are willing to defend, where your limits lie, and what you will do when forced to act. The mentally resilient individual trains not just their muscles but also their conviction, rehearsing their personal line in the sand until it is unmistakably clear.

Managing fear is central to mental readiness. Fear is not an enemy; it is a survival ally. However, when left unchecked, fear can paralyze and blind. Techniques such as box breathing, grounding, and self-talk transform fear into focus. By learning to control your breath, you harness the single most available conscious tool in a crisis. A few deep, deliberate breaths can steady hands, sharpen sight, and preserve rational thought. Rather than suppressing fear, the prepared individual channels it into awareness and purposeful action.

True preparedness must also include a sober understanding of the law and its consequences. Defensive action is not an abstract fantasy but a legal and moral reality. Carrying a weapon or employing force requires knowledge of what is justified, what is excessive, and what the potential aftermath may be. The mentally prepared individual studies local self-defense statutes, learns use-of-force continuums, and anticipates the emotional and legal burdens that may arise afterward. Preparation does not end when the threat flees; it continues through statements to law enforcement, possible court appearances, and the emotional recovery that follows.

When firearms enter the equation, mental clarity becomes even more paramount. A firearm offers unmatched ability to counter lethal threats, especially for those at physical disadvantage, but it demands responsibility at the highest level. Preparedness here means not only marksmanship but decision-making under pressure. It means practicing shoot/no-shoot scenarios, force-on-force simulations, and verbal commands. It means cultivating the discipline to de-escalate whenever possible and to draw only as a last resort. Competence with a firearm is as much about knowing when not to use it as learning how to use it.

Adaptability crowns the skills of the mind and body. Real confrontations are fluid, unpredictable, and messy; the rigid plan crumbles when conditions shift. Adaptability means transitioning seamlessly from verbal de-escalation to physical defense, from grappling to striking, from evasion to confrontation, as the moment requires. Training that incorporates surprise, dynamic environments, and evolving objectives builds the mental agility to shift strategies quickly. The adaptable individual is not locked into one tool or tactic but sees multiple pathways to safety and survival.

Preparedness extends beyond the event itself into recovery. Surviving the moment is not the end; the aftermath may weigh heavier. Psychological effects, trauma, legal scrutiny, and public exposure can follow. The resilient individual anticipates this, securing support systems in advance by preparing trusted legal counsel, counseling resources, and a strong personal network. Just as one trains for the fight, one must also prepare for the days and weeks after, when the mind and heart seek stability again. True defense is measured not only by survival in the moment but by the ability to return to normalcy without being consumed by the incident.

Physical and mental readiness require constant reassessment. Bodies age, minds shift, circumstances change. The training regimen that was sufficient five years ago may no longer be effective. Regular evaluation of strength, speed, reflexes, and decision-making keeps preparedness current. Adaptation is itself a form of training, involving the modification of equipment, refinement of techniques, or adjustment of strategies to match the reality of one's evolving abilities.

Lifestyle supports all of this. Nutrition, hydration, sleep, and stress management are the soil in which readiness grows. Poor health can sabotage reflexes, cloud judgment, and erode resilience. Living with purpose means maintaining balance, not paranoia, but intentionally caring for the body and mind. Recovery, rest, and restoration are just as crucial, if not more so, than drills and workouts. Readiness is not a sprint, but a prolonged and sustained posture of living.

Ultimately, the deepest reservoir of mental preparedness often stems from a purpose that transcends oneself. Many individuals train not only to survive but to protect family, loved ones, and those who cannot defend themselves. That sense of duty amplifies resolve. The parent protecting a child, the partner shielding a spouse, and the protector defending the vulnerable are roles that intensify determination and focus when fear might otherwise overwhelm. Purpose gives courage direction, and in moments of crisis, it can be the decisive factor that compels action instead of paralysis.

Physical conditioning and mental preparedness together form the bedrock of self-defense. They are not destinations but ongoing journeys, cultivated through discipline, humility, repetition, and self-awareness. The story of Mike illustrates the fruits of such preparation, but the principle is universal: in the face of danger, your body and mind will default to their level of training. If you have trained them to be strong, resilient, and clear, you carry into that moment not just hope but hard-earned capacity. In that capacity lies the power to endure, to resist, to survive, and most importantly, to return safely home.

CHAPTER 4

THE ANATOMY OF AWARENESS

Ashley had been the human resources coordinator at a logistics company for six years. She wasn't part of the security or safety staff. Yet, she took both subjects seriously, especially after attending a corporate seminar on workplace violence and threat assessment just a few months earlier. The seminar left her with a sharper sense of observation and a heightened sense of responsibility. Since then, she had begun to notice things most people brushed off without a second thought. Subtle shifts in tone. Withdrawn behavior. Odd comments that didn't sit right. She even collaborated with the legal department to refine the company's incident reporting protocols, making them more transparent, more protective, and easier to follow.

When Tyler, a warehouse technician in his early fifties, began acting strangely, Ashley saw the warning signs. Tyler had once been known for his sense of humor, which was occasionally abrasive but usually sociable and well-liked by his peers. Over the past month, however, that image had eroded. He no longer ate lunch with the team. He began arriving late, staying long after his shift was over, and his once neat appearance gave way to a disheveled, vacant look. His behavior grew erratic. He slammed boxes harder than necessary, muttered under his breath when approached, and even walked away mid-conversation. Individually, these behaviors might have seemed minor, but together they signaled an unsettling shift. It was as if Tyler were slowly isolating himself on an island of frustration.

Coworkers shrugged it off as stress. His manager thought it was burnout. Ashley knew better. She had been trained to look past the surface and examine the patterns. What truly unsettled her were the things she saw on Tyler's public social media accounts. His posts had shifted dramatically. Where once he shared pictures of motorcycles, fishing trips, and classic cars, his tone had grown darker. A recent post read, "Some people deserve what's coming to them." Another showed a photograph of the company's time clock with the caption, "Tick. Tock." He joined discussions about workplace injustice, where his words grew increasingly hostile. These were no longer harmless frustrations. They were red flags.

Ashley compiled everything she had noticed. She didn't exaggerate or speculate. She simply presented the facts: behavioral changes concerning online activity, and two written complaints from coworkers who admitted they felt unsafe around him but hadn't wanted to cause trouble. She presented her findings to the internal safety team, along with a recommendation to conduct a wellness check, temporarily place Tyler on leave, and provide him with resources to support his well-being. It was not punishment. It was prevention.

The safety team acted. With the help of a third-party threat management consultant, they called Tyler in for a meeting. He was quiet but not shocked. He admitted he had been struggling. A recent divorce had left him angry, ashamed, and lost. He confessed that he had been drinking heavily and often felt like snapping, though he insisted he had no specific plan to hurt anyone.

The company placed him on administrative leave, required him to undergo counseling, and mandated a return-to-work evaluation before any possible reinstatement. Security at the warehouse was quietly increased, but staff were not alarmed through unnecessary announcements. Later, Tyler chose not to return. He found another job closer to his brother and eventually emailed Ashley. He thanked her, writing that he hadn't realized how far he had slipped until someone noticed. He admitted she may have saved him from doing something stupid and irreversible.

Ashley sat with his words for a long time. There had been no drama, no whispering rumor mill, no public panic; just careful observation, steady documentation, and timely action. A process rooted in prevention rather than reaction had changed the outcome entirely. It could have ended in disaster. Instead, it ended quietly, with a chance for recovery.

In the weeks that followed, Ashley helped build a more formal threat assessment protocol for the company. Social media monitoring was added to annual background checks. Anonymous reporting was encouraged. Managers were trained to spot early indicators of distress or aggression. She was careful not to create a culture of paranoia but instead to nurture a culture of awareness. The lesson was simple. Danger doesn't always roar; sometimes it whispers.

Threat assessment is the disciplined practice of identifying, analyzing, and prioritizing potential dangers. It is about understanding not only what threats exist, but how they manifest and how to respond before they escalate. Effective threat assessment looks both outward and inward. External threats may come from specific individuals, unsafe locations, social unrest, or criminal activity. Internal threats may originate from within ourselves and our organizations, including denial, overconfidence, or complacency. Both require equal attention if the goal is to build a truly protective framework.

The first step is to apply a structure that organizes the chaos into something measurable and manageable. One of the most valuable systems is the CARVER matrix, which originated in military planning but is now widely used in business, law enforcement, and civilian safety. CARVER stands for Criticality, Accessibility, Recuperability, Vulnerability, Effect, and Recognizability. By breaking down risks into these six categories, vague worries transform into clear priorities. Each factor can be examined, scored, and compared, creating a rational basis for decision-making rather than relying on guesswork.

Criticality refers to the importance or value of a potential target. For civilians, this means asking how significant the impact would be if that target were compromised. A family member's daily commute is critical because their safety is central to the household, whereas a storage shed in the backyard is far less critical. By identifying what is most vital, you determine what must be protected first.

Accessibility examines how easily someone with harmful intent can reach a target. At home, this could mean unlocked doors, windows hidden by overgrown bushes, or predictable routines that expose you at the same time and place every day. Recognizing accessibility forces you to confront patterns of exposure and make adjustments to reduce predictability.

Recuperability addresses how quickly you can recover if a target is attacked. Do you have backups of important documents? Do you have insurance for valuable possessions? If your only copies of vital records are kept in a single drawer, your recuperability is low. Building redundancy enhances resilience and facilitates faster recovery from setbacks.

Vulnerability is the measure of weaknesses that make a target easier to exploit. Unlike accessibility, which focuses on exposure, vulnerability emphasizes how easy it is to succeed once an attack is attempted. Weak locks, poor lighting, lack of defensive training, or traveling alone in unsafe areas all create vulnerability. Identifying these weaknesses points directly to where improvements are most needed.

Effect measures the broader consequences of an attack. Losing a primary vehicle does not just mean temporary inconvenience; it may lead to missed work, lost income, and household stress. Evaluating the effect allows you to understand the ripple effects of an incident and weigh which risks would cause the most disruption if realized.

Recognizability refers to the ease with which an attacker can identify a target. Flashing large sums of money in public, posting expensive possessions online, or leaving tools in plain sight make you more recognizable as an easy target. A poorly maintained home that looks unoccupied may draw burglars. By viewing your environment through the eyes of a predator, you learn to minimize signals that attract unwanted attention.

When combined, these six factors provide a comprehensive picture of areas that should be prioritized. A target that is highly critical but well secured may not be as urgent to address as something less critical but easily accessible and highly vulnerable.

Individuals can score each factor on a scale of 1 to 10, creating a chart that ranks risks in order of urgency. This transforms fear into strategy.

Applied to a home, CARVER reveals where defenses must be strengthened; bedrooms, where family members sleep, rank high in criticality, while a backyard shed ranks low in importance. Accessibility asks whether doors and windows are secured and whether the property is visible from the street. Recuperability assesses whether backups of documents and insurance coverage are available. Vulnerability assesses the strength of locks and doors. The effect considers the degree of disruption a break-in would cause. Recognizability assesses whether the home appears lived-in or abandoned. By scoring each category, homeowners can identify areas where to invest energy, such as stronger locks, better lighting, or building redundancies.

The power of CARVER lies in its ability to turn reactive thinking into a proactive strategy. Most people only consider safety after something has already gone wrong. CARVER enables you to identify vulnerabilities before they are exploited and address them with forethought. It offers a structured, disciplined approach that builds resilience, deters opportunistic attacks, and fosters confidence.

Risk management is the natural extension of threat assessment. Once risks are identified, the task becomes reducing them. Risk management means eliminating hazards whenever possible, reducing exposure when elimination is not feasible, and preparing responses for situations when confrontation is unavoidable. It may involve adjusting travel routes, upgrading home security, or avoiding specific areas at certain times of day. Risk management distinguishes the reactive from the proactive.

A thorough risk assessment includes geography and social dynamics. Where you live and work directly shapes the risks you face. Urban areas may have higher rates of theft, robbery, or gang violence. Rural areas may pose risks of delayed emergency response or environmental dangers. Social dynamics, from economic stress to political unrest, also influence threat levels. Your personal circumstances, such as age, gender, profession, and lifestyle, also shape your vulnerabilities.

Situational context must always be considered. A park may be safe at noon, but it can be dangerous at midnight. A gas station may seem routine on a weekday, but it can become a target late at night. Threat-aware individuals continually adjust their perception in response to changing conditions. This skill grows with experience, awareness, and scenario planning.

Threat assessment also requires an honest evaluation of personal lifestyle factors. Substance abuse, financial instability, toxic relationships, or careless online behavior can all expose vulnerabilities. Oversharing personal details on social media can put you at risk of being stalked or targeted by thieves. Clothing, vehicles, or behavior that signals wealth can make you a target. Reducing unnecessary signals reduces risk.

Technology provides valuable tools, from surveillance systems to safety apps, but it must be used wisely. Overreliance can create a false sense of security. Tools must complement awareness, not replace it. Training, drills, and scenario-based exercises ensure that technology is integrated into a living, practical system rather than becoming a crutch.

Effective risk management also includes contingency planning. This means having escape routes, emergency contacts, defensive tools, and medical supplies ready. Every environment, from home to work, vehicle, and public spaces, should have a well-thought-out plan for emergencies.

Threat assessment does not stop with the individual. Parents must assess schools and childcare centers. Spouses and partners should remain aware of each other's routines. Shared vigilance and family safety plans build collective resilience.

Another critical dimension is understanding the psychology of predators. Attackers often test boundaries before striking. They may use charm, intimidation, or manipulation to disarm or probe potential victims. Recognizing these behaviors enables the early identification of threats and facilitates timely responses.

Community plays a powerful role. Neighborhoods where residents look out for each other tend to deter crime. Isolation and neglect invite it. Engaging with neighbors, advocating for lighting or surveillance, and participating in safety networks multiply the strength of individual vigilance.

Social media must also be handled carefully. Real-time posts about travel plans or expensive purchases create easy opportunities for predators. Risk management requires discretion and a delayed approach to sharing.

Insider threats must be considered. Sometimes danger comes from within trusted circles. Workplace violence, domestic abuse, or betrayal by acquaintances are particularly dangerous because they bypass normal defenses. These require documentation, secure boundaries, and often legal intervention.

Legal risks cannot be ignored. Every act of self-defense must comply with laws on the use of force. Misjudging legality can lead to criminal charges or civil liability. Risk management involves understanding the laws of your location and consulting with legal experts regularly to stay informed.

The design of physical environments can significantly reduce risk. Crime Prevention Through Environmental Design (CPTED) is a concept that emphasizes the use of lighting, sightlines, barriers, and regular maintenance to deter criminal behavior. A well-kept, visible, and reinforced space sends a message of protection.

Layering defenses ensures redundancy. Instead of relying on a single measure, multiple layers create time and options: alarms, locks, barriers, animals, cameras, defensive tools, and medical readiness. Each layer strengthens the overall system.

Preparation must include rare but high-impact events. Active shooter incidents, terrorist attacks, natural disasters, or home invasions may be unlikely, but their consequences are severe. Drills, escape plans, and emergency kits can make the difference between chaos and a controlled response.

The ultimate goal of threat assessment and risk management is to live with awareness, not fear. It means moving through the world with eyes open, prepared to respond, but free to enjoy life with confidence. It means treating threats as solvable problems rather than inevitabilities.

After any incident, post-event reflection is essential. Reviewing what worked and what failed refines the process and strengthens resilience. Every confrontation becomes an opportunity to learn and improve.

Threat assessment and risk management are never complete. They are ongoing, dynamic processes requiring vigilance, honesty, and discipline. They do not encourage paranoia. They build preparedness for anticipated possibilities. They are not about hiding from or fearing the world. They are about living fully, freely, and safely, with the awareness and tools needed to protect yourself and those you love.

CHAPTER 5

PRINCIPLES OF DEFENSIVE ACTION

Matt had always prided himself on being composed behind the wheel. He was the kind of driver who let others merge without complaint, waved to pedestrians as they crossed, and preferred to keep an interesting podcast playing instead of blaring music. However, one Friday evening, the city was gridlocked with pre-weekend traffic, and the tension seemed to hang in the air like heavy fog. Matt just wanted to get home before dark, but every driver around him seemed to have the same urgency, and patience was running low.

As he approached an intersection, the yellow light ahead lingered a little too long. Matt tapped the brakes and slowed to a careful stop. Just as he did, a black pickup truck behind him surged forward and barely avoided colliding with his bumper. The horn blared, long and angry, echoing through the line of cars. Matt glanced in his rearview mirror and saw the driver's face, red with fury, shouting something inaudible, fists pounding the steering wheel as if each strike could shatter a walnut.

PRINCIPLES OF DEFENSIVE ACTION

Matt's first instinct was irritation. He had done nothing wrong, and yet this stranger was acting as though he had been wronged. Before he could process the thought, the truck swerved beside him into the empty turn lane. The driver, a large middle-aged man with thick arms and an even thicker scowl, rolled down his passenger window and began shouting directly at Matt. His gestures were inflammatory, his voice cracked with rage, and every muscle in his body seemed coiled for confrontation. Other drivers were beginning to notice. A few honked, some stared, and others quietly maneuvered around the two vehicles to escape the brewing storm.

The light turned green.

Matt felt his heart begin to race, the pulse ticking like a drum in his throat. He could feel the pull of his pride, the temptation to roll down his own window and shout back. After all, he had every right to argue his side. He had obeyed the law, he had done nothing wrong, and here was a man unleashing unprovoked hostility upon him, but in that split second, another thought surfaced. He remembered a conversation with his sister, an emergency room nurse, who had often shared stories with him about angry patients and frustrated family members. She once said to him, "Don't let them suck you into their anger. You never know what someone else is carrying or how far they are willing to go." That memory struck him like a dodgeball.

So instead of shouting back, Matt took a slow breath. He turned his head and looked over, not with anger, but with calmness in his eyes. His hands remained visible on the wheel, his posture relaxed, his movements measured. No clenched fists, no aggressive gestures. He gave the man a slight nod and spoke in a tone so steady it surprised even him. "Sorry about that, sir."

The driver seemed caught off guard. That was not the reaction he expected. He was looking forward to a verbal war, maybe even physical violence, but instead, he was met with words that carried no venom. Matt continued, his voice even, his tone calm, "I didn't want to accidentally blow through a red light. Just trying to get home safe, again, sorry about the stop."

There was a pause. The man's face twisted as if ready to spit another insult, but the volume dropped. He muttered something under his breath, shook his head, and then sat back against his seat. The fury seemed to lose momentum, anger's fire seemed deprived of oxygen. Matt looked forward, the light still green, and eased into the intersection with steady movements. He did not glare into the mirror. He did not slam the gas pedal in defiance. He simply drove and gradually accelerated to the speed limit.

A few blocks later, the pickup turned off down a side street. Matt continued toward home, realizing only as he pulled into his driveway how tight his shoulders had been. He exhaled, letting the tension bleed out of him. For a moment, he sat in the car, thinking about how differently the encounter could have ended. If he had matched the man's rage, the situation might have spiraled into a violent confrontation. If he had shouted back, the man might have followed him home, or worse, and if that man had accessed a traditional or improvised weapon, a reckless decision made in the heat of the moment could have cost Matt his life. Instead, by choosing still waters over fire, he had prevented the encounter from escalating.

He never told the story that night. There was no need to. Nothing dramatic had happened. No punches thrown, no car chases, no sirens. However, beneath the surface, something significant had occurred. A volatile situation had been cooled

PRINCIPLES OF DEFENSIVE ACTION

because one man refused to let his ego dictate his response. In that small act of restraint lay the most frequent and typical path of self-defense, not always in striking, grappling, overpowering, or engaging in a gunfight, but in choosing to de-escalate and disengage.

De-escalation is the art of lowering the tension in a confrontation or incident. It is not a sign of weakness, nor is it passive. It is active, deliberate, and deeply strategic. Every confrontation we encounter, whether in traffic, in public, at work, or even at home, requires de-escalation. The methods may differ depending on the circumstances, but the goal remains the same: prevent violence, protect life, and resolve conflict with the least harm possible.

De-escalation can take many forms. Sometimes, it is using our words to calm and diffuse an individual, just as Matt did with the road-raged driver. Sometimes, it is necessary to remove ourselves from the situation entirely, choosing distance over debate, and in extreme cases, such as facing an active shooter, de-escalation cannot be achieved solely through words or body language. It must come through decisive defensive action, such as the lawful use of a firearm to stop a deadly threat. The method changes with the context, but the principle remains the same: de-escalation is always the first priority, because every confrontation needs to end or be avoided before it gets worse.

At the heart of verbal de-escalation lies communication. Words, tone, posture, eye contact, and body language all act as signals that either calm or inflame. A hostile stance, a mocking tone, or dismissive words will almost always escalate, even if that is not the intent. On the other hand, open hands, a calm voice, measured eye contact, and a non-threatening stance project safety.

The aggressor's mind, already clouded by anger or fear, looks for signals of threat or dominance. By refusing to feed those signals, you strip their hostility of fuel.

However, beyond technique lies psychology, and at the center of human aggression are powerful drivers: ego, pride, and humiliation. More conflicts are sparked and sustained by wounded pride than by actual physical harm. When people feel disrespected, embarrassed, or made to look weak, they often lash out to reclaim their sense of control. Ego demands recognition, pride resists shame, and humiliation seeks revenge. This is why so many confrontations spiral out of control in public places where others can witness them; the aggressor feels they cannot back down without losing face. Wise individuals understand this truth and act accordingly.

Preserving the other person's dignity, even when they are in the wrong, can be one of the most effective tools in de-escalation. If you can allow them an exit that does not leave them humiliated, they are far more likely to disengage. This may mean swallowing your own pride, resisting the urge to prove you are right, or avoiding sarcastic comebacks that would make you feel superior. It takes humility to let someone else feel as though they have "won" when you know the real victory lies in avoiding violence. Still, this preservation of dignity can diffuse a situation faster than any clever rebuttal. When you guard your own ego while safeguarding theirs, you create a pathway for a peaceful resolution.

The failure to manage ego often explains why small arguments escalate into deadly encounters. A spilled drink at a bar can escalate into a fistfight because someone feels disrespected. A minor traffic dispute turns into road rage because one driver refused to let the other "get away with it." Even domestic arguments can spiral out of control when one person refuses to step back, determined to have the last word. Recognizing ego as a fuel source of conflict allows you to remove that fuel by refusing to participate in the competition. You do not have to agree with the aggressor, but you can acknowledge their feelings in a way that preserves their sense of self. "I see you're upset, and I'm sorry I worded it that way" is not a surrender; it is a strategy.

This concept is closely tied to what some refer to as "verbal judo." Instead of pushing against someone's aggression with equal or greater aggression, you blend with it, redirect it, and gently guide it in a different direction. Like a martial artist deflecting a strike, you absorb the emotional energy without letting it hit you directly. For example, if someone shouts, "You think you're more important than the rest of us?" a defensive answer fuels the fire, but replying, "No, not at all. I'm sorry I didn't realize I was parked over the line and taking up two spots. Sorry about that, I'll move my car," sidesteps the accusation while calming the tone. It grants the aggressor dignity, validates their feelings without validating their aggression, and gives them a chance to back down gracefully.

Tone can be medicinal or weaponized depending on how it is used. A sharp command can inflame, while a calm suggestion can soothe. Even your breathing influences the exchange. Slow, deep breaths not only calm your own nervous system but can also affect the aggressor subconsciously, encouraging them to mirror your pace. Controlled breathing, calm voice, and relaxed posture all combine to project stability, and stability is often contagious.

The physical aspects of de-escalation, including space and proximity, are just as vital. Standing too close can feel like a threat, while stepping back slightly can ease the pressure. Placing a physical barrier, such as a chair or table, between yourself and the aggressor buys both time and space without appearing aggressive. Positioning yourself near an exit gives you the option to leave if necessary, while still maintaining a calm and conversational stance. This management of space, known as proxemics, allows you to reduce the risk of physical harm while still working toward resolution.

Of course, not every situation allows for calm words or subtle body language. Some individuals are beyond the reach of verbal persuasion. Intoxication, mental instability, extreme rage, or criminal intent may render communication useless. In those moments, disengagement becomes the best form of de-escalation. Walking away, retreating, or escaping the situation entirely is not cowardice; it is a form of survival. The goal is not to win an argument but to get home safe. Recognizing when to disengage is as critical as knowing how to speak calmly.

Yet there are rare but severe scenarios when disengagement is impossible and communication is ineffective - such as encountering an active shooter or other imminent deadly threat. In those moments, de-escalation takes its final form: lawful, decisive defensive action. Stopping a lethal threat through appropriate force is not escalation; it is the ultimate act of de-escalation, because it prevents further harm and ends the confrontation. Just as words or space can reduce danger, so too can a defensive response when lives are immediately at stake. The principle remains unchanged: end the threat, preserve life, and bring the conflict to a close.

De-escalation, then, is not a single tactic but a spectrum of responses. It can be as simple as keeping your voice calm in a heated argument, as strategic as preserving someone's dignity to defuse their anger, as tactical as creating physical distance in a confrontation, or as decisive as using defensive skills and tools to stop a deadly threat. The unifying thread is always the same: reduce harm, prevent violence, and resolve the situation with the least damage possible.

Ultimately, de-escalation requires discipline, humility, and maturity. It demands that we control not only the situation but ourselves. By mastering our own emotions, refusing to let ego dictate our actions, and preserving the dignity of others, we create space for peace even in the shadow of conflict. It may not feel heroic in the moment, but there is no greater victory than walking away safe, having transformed potential violence into nothing more than silence. In the truest sense, de-escalation is not only a skill, it is the highest expression of defensive understanding.

CHAPTER 6

TOOLS WITH PURPOSE

Emily had never once thought about being a hero. She was the sort of woman who quietly slipped a few extra dollars into the donation box, remembered her neighbor's birthday with homemade bread, and stayed behind after community events to stack chairs long after everyone else had gone home. But she carried several items on her person, including a tourniquet in her pocket every day. It wasn't part of some tactical routine or identity; it was just something that made sense to her. She'd taken a "Stop the Bleed" class after a coworker lost a finger in a warehouse accident and had been stunned at how fragile the human body really was. The instructor had told the class that a person could bleed out from a femoral artery that has been severed in less than three minutes, and that even the best EMS response couldn't consistently beat that clock. She'd gone home that night, ordered a quality tourniquet online, and started carrying it in her front pocket with her keys. It became a habit so small she hardly noticed it anymore, a quiet token of preparation that followed her everywhere. Months passed without incident, the way they often do when you're prepared, until one cold afternoon when everything changed in the space between two heartbeats.

She had been driving home after picking up groceries when the truck ahead of her swerved sharply to avoid a dog darting into the road. It missed the animal but overcorrected, clipping the shoulder and flipping. The sound was terrible, a sharp metallic snap followed by the crunching roll of glass and steel. She stopped immediately, decisive action overriding deep analysis, and jumped out of her car. The overturned vehicle had come to rest on its roof, one tire still spinning. The driver's window was shattered, and inside, a man was slumped sideways against the ceiling, legs twisted awkwardly against the dash. Blood was running fast down one thigh, pooling beneath him in a spreading sheet.

Emily called out to him, got no response, and knelt by the window. Training, long practiced and barely remembered, kicked in. She tore off his jacket, ducked low, and slid inside far enough to reach the man's beltline. The wound was deep; she saw spurting each time the man's heart pulsed weakly. There was no time to think about causes or complications. She pulled the tourniquet from her pocket, looped it high on the leg, tightened it until the bleeding stopped, and locked the windlass. Then Emily checked the man's breathing, still there but shallow, and called 911 with the other hand. The dispatcher stayed on the line while she gave calm, articulate answers. The minutes stretched long, but she didn't feel them. She just held pressure, monitored the tourniquet, and kept the man talking once consciousness flickered back. When the ambulance arrived, the medics moved quickly, cutting away the patient's clothing, checking his vitals, and attending to his needs. One of them looked up and said, "You saved his life."

Later, after the chaos had passed, Emily sat in her car shaking, the delayed tremor of adrenaline settling into her limbs. She thought about how simple the whole thing was, how small that piece of nylon and plastic had been, how light it was in her pocket, how unnoticeable, how ordinary, and yet it had made all the difference. She realized that day that preparedness isn't about dramatics or equipment hoarding; it's about accessibility and consistency. It's about what you can get to when the seconds matter, and what you've trained yourself to do when thought is replaced by action.

That story could belong to anyone. You don't have to be a medic, a police officer, or a soldier to be capable of decisive action. You only have to decide, in advance, that your safety and the safety of others are worth a small investment of forethought and habit. That's what the earlier chapters have been building: the belt itself. Now we arrive at the tools that hang on that belt, the physical extensions of all those lessons. The belt is your foundation; the tools are how you extend your reach and achieve a higher capability. The truth is unforgiving but straightforward: in a critical incident, the tools you'll have at your disposal will be dictated entirely by what you made accessible beforehand.

Accessibility is the dividing line between intention and capability. It's one thing to own a flashlight, to have a firearm in a safe, to keep a first-aid kit in a vehicle. It's another to have what you need within reach, on your person, when the emergency is happening right in front of you. There's an old saying in preparedness circles: "If you don't have it on you, you don't have it," and that is true. Emergencies can happen anywhere, not just where you store things. You will fight with what's on you, treat with what's in your hands, and survive with what you've planned for in advance. This is why the foundation of every defensive lifestyle must include carefully chosen, accessible, everyday-carry tools. Not for paranoia. Not for appearance. For readiness.

A person's daily carry, their personal toolbelt, is as individual as their fingerprint. There are no one-size-fits-all answers because what you carry must reflect who you are, where you go, and what you face. The nurse who drives through rural backroads after midnight has different needs than the office worker walking to their car downtown. Still, the principle is universal: your tools must be accessible, functional, and practiced. You don't rise to the level of your fantasy; you fall to the level of your preparation.

For most people, the cornerstone of daily preparedness starts with three basic categories: light, medical, and defense. Light allows you to see and be seen. Medical will enable you to preserve life. Defense allows you to protect it. These are the anchors that balance the belt. A flashlight, though simple, is among the most versatile and underrated tools you can carry. It gives you control over the environment, extending both your perception and your deterrence. In low-light conditions, it identifies threats before they close the distance. In nonviolent moments, it illuminates paths, keys, and safety hazards. In emergencies, it signals for help, blinds an attacker, or allows you to assess an injury. A good light is compact, bright, and designed for one-handed use. It's a universal symbol of readiness that raises no eyebrows but changes everything in a dark environment.

Next comes medical preparedness, the kind that saved the man in the truck. A small tourniquet in your pocket, a pressure bandage, or even a compact trauma dressing are not burdensome items to carry. They weigh less than a phone and take up less space than a wallet, yet they can bridge the gap between injury and survival. Catastrophic bleeding kills faster than almost anything else. You can go days without food, hours without shelter, minutes without air, but you can bleed out in under three. Carrying the means to stop bleeding is one of the purest, most practical expressions of self-reliance and compassion there is. Every person who carries a firearm should also have a tourniquet. Every person who works around tools, drives, or spends time outdoors should do the same. It's not about paranoia, but about potential.

Then there's defense, the subject that most often polarizes but also most clearly defines responsibility. Self-defense tools come in many forms, including both lethal and non-lethal, as well as visible and discreet options. The right choice depends on your comfort level, your environment, legal restrictions, and your willingness to undergo training. For some, that means pepper spray, one of the most accessible and highly effective defensive options available. Properly deployed, it creates distance, incapacitates without killing, and gives you the vital seconds needed to escape. It's inexpensive, compact, and legal in most jurisdictions, though it does require awareness of wind and range. Like every other tool, it must be accessible; if you have to dig for it in your bag, it's less deployable and therefore tougher to utilize effectively.

Others might choose a taser or a stun device. These can be effective when used properly, but must be treated as tools with limitations, not guarantees. Clothing, battery charge, and distance all affect their success. Then comes the firearm, the most decisive tool on the belt, and the one that carries the most significant capacity to equalize the ability to defend. Carrying a firearm for personal defense is not about machismo or fear; it's about recognizing the reality that violence can appear anywhere, and that police response is measured in minutes while survival is measured in seconds. Still, the gun is not the first tool. It is the last. It sits at the far end of the spectrum, reserved for when all else would be ineffective and the threat is immediate and deadly. To carry one ethically means to train relentlessly, to understand the law intimately, and to develop the mental discipline to make a life-and-death decision under stress. A firearm demands not just skill but character. It's not a symbol of power; it's a burden of responsibility.

Regardless of which items you choose, the principle remains the same: accessibility and consistency. The best tool is the one you will actually carry. It must fit seamlessly into your daily life, not appear and disappear on random days or evenings. The minimalist, consistently carrying a flashlight, a folding knife, a handgun, and a tourniquet, is far more prepared than the enthusiast whose bulky rig sits unused at home. Preparedness must be sustainable; otherwise, it isn't real. If it's uncomfortable, inconvenient, or socially awkward to the point that you leave it behind, it fails. The goal is not to carry everything, it's to have what matters most every day.

There's a saying among those who live this lifestyle: "When you carry a gun, you're also carrying a light, a tourniquet, and good judgment." Those four items, the firearm, the flashlight, the medical gear, and the mindset, form a balanced system. They ensure that you're not simply armed, but prepared, not just ready to fight, but ready to save. The world has enough people who carry weapons; it needs more who bring wisdom and discernment with them. Preparedness means being equipped not only to protect life but to preserve it as well.

Training is what turns equipment into ability. Without it, tools become objects that make you feel safe without actually increasing safety. Each tool you carry must be trained with until its use is subconscious. Drawing a light, applying a tourniquet, deploying pepper spray, or presenting a firearm all require practice. Not just practice in isolation, but practice under realistic conditions. Train in the clothes you wear, in the environments you frequent, with the tools you actually carry. The repetition builds familiarity, and familiarity breeds a sense of calm. In crisis, your body will default to its highest level of consistent training, not the lowest level of imagination.

There's also humility in preparedness, a quiet acceptance that you will never be ready for everything. No one is. However, you can be prepared for most things if you discipline yourself to carry, maintain, and train consistently. The temptation, especially among enthusiasts, is to overcomplicate, to carry too much, to seek identity in equipment rather than skill, but the truth is more straightforward and quieter. The more experienced someone becomes, the less they carry. What remains are the essentials: light, medical, defense, and knowledge. The rest is noise. The mature practitioner trims excess until only what's necessary remains.

Preparedness is a lifestyle, not a hobby. It's not something you perform for others; it's something you live for yourself. The person who carries a tourniquet in their pocket doesn't advertise it; they just have it. The woman who keeps pepper spray on her keychain doesn't post about it; she simply knows it's there. The man who carries a concealed firearm does so not out of ego but out of quiet duty to those he loves. It's not about looking the part; it's about being ready when life gives you no warning.

When people first begin this journey, they often think of tools as optional accessories. However, the more you understand real-world emergencies, the more you realize that tools are extensions of your will and your planning. A flashlight is an extension of awareness. A medical kit is an extension of compassion. A defensive tool is an extension of resolve. None of them functions without the human being behind them, but each one multiplies what that human can do when properly used.

Carrying tools daily also changes how you move through the world. It instills mindfulness. You become more observant, more deliberate. You start noticing exits, lighting conditions, crowd behavior, and body language. You stop drifting through life on autopilot and start engaging with it consciously. That awareness alone, even before any physical tool is deployed, prevents countless problems. The truly prepared individual avoids more danger than they ever confront, not because they're lucky, but because they see it coming before it arrives. The tools simply give them a way out when avoidance fails.

All of this exists within balance. It's easy to tip too far toward paranoia or fantasy, to believe you can gear your way out of danger or that carrying a weapon makes you invincible. Still, preparedness isn't about dominance; it's about continuity. It's about ensuring that life goes on. The tools you carry are there to buy time, for police to arrive, for medics to treat, for you to escape or defend, for others to survive. They're not solely about the ending of an incident; they're more about the continuation of life and return to as much normalcy as possible.

What you carry on your person each day is the foundation of your readiness. It's the baseline. The rest, like your vehicle kit, your home setup, or your workplace supplies, builds on it. However, it starts with what's literally at your side when the moment arrives. Light, medical, and defense, balanced with judgment and discipline, form the trinity of everyday carry. Everything beyond that is refinement.

At the end of the day, preparedness isn't about things; it's about people. The tools are inert until animated by purpose. The purpose is simple: to preserve life, protect others, and prevent chaos from claiming those you care about. Although we've spoken here about what you carry on your body as well as the daily tools within reach, there will come a time to expand outward. Unique environments like your vehicle, your workplace, and your home each deserve tailored approaches of their own, because each presents different constraints, risks, and opportunities for accessibility. Those environments, however, all depend on one constant: YOU. The person who carries intelligently, consistently, and with purpose becomes the nucleus of every preparedness plan they inhabit. The gear you wear is only as good as the discipline behind it.

So, when you step into the world, ask yourself one question: if something happened right now, what would I have in reach? Not what's in your trunk, not what's on a shelf, but what's on you, what you've chosen to make part of your daily life. Since the world will not wait for you to fetch your tools, it will hand you the test before you can study. The prepared don't guess; they act not through the obsession with catastrophe, but the quiet, steady confidence of knowing that if fate calls your name, your hands won't be empty.

CHAPTER 7

THE STRONGHOLD: HOME AND VEHICLE PREPAREDNESS

Jake lived in a modest home on the edge of town, close enough to the rural backroads that he could disappear into the trees if he needed to, but not so isolated that he felt cut off from the pulse of the world. That evening, the horizon had turned the color of lead, clouds rolling with the promise of violence. The weather alerts had been coming across every station for hours, urging residents to shelter in place and expect widespread outages. But Jake was calm. He'd seen storms before. He knew that what most people feared wasn't just the wind or the rain, it was the unknown that followed. When the lights went out and the familiar hum of civilization faded, people changed. Some grew quiet and patient. Others grew desperate. The memory of the nights after the last storm informed everything he did now. He had seen how people shifted when the lights went out and the noise of rescue and order thinned; some became thoughtful neighbors, others opportunists who tested doors and screens until someone had to shout. That recollection was the reason he moved early, methodically, and without panic. He bolted shutters, stacked sandbags along a low slope in the yard, and ran the generator until its steady hum promised electricity. He flung tarps over patio furniture, made sure garden tools were out of sight in the shed, and filled bathtubs for sanitation, but he also thought about how the house met the world beyond the fence. At dusk, he inspected locking hardware, made a quick modification to a sliding door with a removable interior bar, and confirmed that motion lights and cameras were functional. He placed a small tote by the interior door with headlamps, batteries, spare phone chargers, a compact trauma kit, and a printed list of emergency contact numbers. He checked the vehicle one last time, verifying the fuel level, tire pressure, and a compact roadside kit under the seat. He felt a sense of relief, knowing that the systems were not fragile because they had been thoroughly considered beforehand. The family gathered in the interior room they had practiced moving to days earlier, and when the storm arrived, they slept in shifts while the radio played local advisories and the generator hummed like a patient animal. In the morning, the yard was scattered with the storm's aftermath: shingles, branches, a twisted patio chair, but the house and the people inside remained. A neighbor whose home had suffered more extensive damage was given coffee and an offer to recharge a phone, because, to Jake, preparedness was never just about isolated survival; it was about being an asset in a neighborhood that could respond together.

That scene is offered as a starting point because preparedness begins in narrative, in the story you tell yourself about what you will do when things go wrong, and because it shows the interplay of three distinct but interdependent elements: the person, the vehicle, and the home. Each element has its capabilities and its limitations, and the art of readiness lies in arranging them so each

THE STRONGHOLD: HOME AND VEHICLE PREPAREDNESS

compensates for what the others cannot do alone. Imagine this relationship in medical terms: you as the individual are the paramedic with immediate capability and mobility, your vehicle is the ambulance carrying extended capability and acting as the bridge, and the home is the hospital where long-duration sustainment, deeper medical care, and recovery occur. Framed this way, every purchase, every placement of gear, every decision about storage, training, or strategy becomes part of a coherent system rather than a collection of isolated items. The paramedic cannot carry everything needed for recovery; the ambulance contains supplies and equipment that the paramedic cannot carry for long; and the hospital supplies the infrastructure and prolonged care. In the same vein, the person will carry what is immediately necessary for action and survival during a brief movement or initial threat, the vehicle will be equipped with things that cannot be worn all day but are essential for extended field support or transport, and the home will carry the deeper stores, the energy infrastructure, and secure, organized systems for sustaining a family and providing refuge to others.

Thinking in systems changes the way you stock, store, and practice. On your person you prioritize items that are lightweight, rapidly accessible, and tailored to mobility: a reliable flashlight or headlamp that frees your hands, a multi-tool that handles improvised problems, a compact med kit intended for immediate stabilization, and communicative means that fit your daily habits such as a charged phone with a power-efficient radio app or a small, handheld radio if you use that network. The weight of everyday carry must be considered carefully; not everything is worth carrying every hour of the day, so design that kit to be surgical in its purpose: what will you absolutely need in the first ten to thirty minutes when events change without warning? Think in terms of stabilization, immediate situational awareness, and the ability to move.

The vehicle is where capability grows. Unlike a person, the car can hold heavier, bulkier items that provide endurance and solve logistical challenges. In the vehicle, you can maintain a full trauma bag with multiple tourniquets, compressive gauze, a hemostatic dressing, airway adjuncts, and supplies to manage a serious bleed until professional care is reached.. You can store spare water in food-grade containers and use simple filtration systems or purification tablets to treat water found on the road. Tools such as a quality jack and spare tire, jumper cables, a tow strap, and a compact toolkit are not glamorous but will keep mobility when the margin for error narrows. The truck or SUV can carry a secure lockbox for firearms that must be stored and transported lawfully and securely, and it can also host a portable power station or solar folding panel, allowing you to recharge communications gear, run a small fridge for medicines that require regulated temperatures, or keep medical devices functioning. It can also serve as a logistics point for heat: a compact propane heater, intended for outdoor use, can help maintain warmth for short periods when sheltered outside the vehicle, and a collection of blankets, sleeping pads, and spare clothing makes prolonged movement more bearable. The vehicle is the ideal location for staging a larger kit for longer events, including more substantial food stores, a small folding shovel and tarp for shelter, cordage, and a fixed rope or strap for moving debris or securing tarps. Keep these items organized so they can be quickly transferred from trunk to cabin; use labeled, durable containers or vehicle-specific storage solutions like cargo organizers and locking trunks. The truck becomes a mobile ambulance, increasing the length of time and distance over which you can act.

THE STRONGHOLD: HOME AND VEHICLE PREPAREDNESS

The home is the hospital in this metaphor: it holds the infrastructure that sustains life when the outside world fails. Water storage and collection systems are a priority because nothing sustains a household like safe water. Rain capture using food-grade barrels and a simple overflow diverter, or cisterns if you have the space and budget, reduces dependency on municipal systems. Secondary filtration systems, paired with bottled water reserves, allow you to weather weeks without resupply. Power redundancy is essential; a generator provides immediate backup for short-term outages, but a layered approach that includes a battery bank with an inverter and a modest solar array reduces fuel dependence and offers a quiet, long-duration option for maintaining critical electronics, lighting, and refrigeration for meds or food. Position the solar panels where shading is minimal, and consider installing a transfer switch that allows you to safely tie the generator's output into your home's panel, in accordance with electrical code. Fuel storage, if you choose to keep it, must adhere to strict safety protocols, including the use of approved containers, cool, shaded storage, and awareness of local regulations. Your home's ability to keep food safe, produce hot water, provide light, and run medical devices can make the difference between a tolerable inconvenience and a dangerous collapse of well-being.

Security in the home is both physical and procedural. Reinforcing exterior doors, extending screws into the door frame, and installing strike plates of sufficient strength are low-gloss tasks with high returns. Windows can be treated with security film or shuttered to deny easy entry, and sliding doors can be fitted with interior bars or removable rods. The garage is often overlooked as a soft target; reinforcing the interior door, securing the garage door with a slide bolt or crossbar, and controlling remote openers are simple yet effective precautions. Defensive layout also means creating clear sightlines around the house so movement near the perimeter is visible from inside; that might mean pruning dense shrubbery, relocating large objects away from entryways, and positioning exterior lights so they illuminate approach routes rather than producing blind spots. Lighting should be layered, with soft, steady lighting for general movement, supplemented by motion-activated lights in key approaches and pathways to highlight and draw attention to movement. Cameras can deter and document, but they are not substitutes for solid mechanical security. They should be configured with strong passwords, placed to record approaches and egress paths, and integrated into a plan that includes off-site backups or local storage that cannot be casually destroyed. Consider placing a small, well-organized command area inside the home, such as a table or binder, where maps, a printed contact list, a physical checklist of supplies, spare batteries, portable chargers, and written family roles are kept and reviewed, allowing for expedited decision-making under stress.

Medical preparation at home should be more comprehensive than a single first-aid kit; it should extend to a staged approach where immediate stabilization items exist on the person and in the vehicle, and more capable trauma and support supplies reside in the home. A home kit might include multiple tourniquets, hemostatic dressings, trauma dressings, compressive wraps, airway adjuncts, splints, burn care supplies, and a stock of over-the-counter medications for pain and infection prevention. It should be accompanied by printed medical histories of household members and a list of critical medications, doses, and known allergies. Training transforms supplies into life-saving interventions: at least two household members should know CPR and basic bleeding control, and ideally attend periodic refreshers. The psychological element cannot be overstated; practicing the

THE STRONGHOLD: HOME AND VEHICLE PREPAREDNESS

application of a tourniquet, for instance, reduces the hesitation that can be fatal in an actual emergency. Just as importantly, have arrangements for the storage of temperature-sensitive meds, including a small medical refrigerator powered by your backup system or a plan for the rapid transfer of meds to alternate care facilities.

Communication is the nervous system of preparedness. While modern life depends on cell phones, those networks can fail. A layered approach to communications should include battery-powered radios tuned to local emergency broadcasts, the option for an amateur radio or GMRS handheld if you or a neighbor is licensed and trained, and a plan to use the vehicle's radio or a dash-mounted antenna when a longer range is needed. Keep hard copies of emergency numbers and meeting points in a waterproof binder, and prearrange an out-of-area contact who can serve as a communications hub should local lines become congested. Post-event communication is not just about calling for help; it's about coordinating movement, alerting neighbors, and keeping morale steady. Teach family members how to send concise status messages, including their name, location, status, and any immediate needs. In the absence of networks, little pieces of paper placed in agreed locations or the use of physical signal methods can be part of a redundant communication plan.

Storage and organization are the unsung heroes of a system. Equipment that is scattered becomes useless when seconds count; organized caches enable rapid access and reduce cognitive load. In the home, allocate defined spaces for food, water, medical, and defensive loadouts that are clearly labeled and routinely checked. Rotate food and water regularly to prevent expiration, document inventories, and maintain a simple log for battery replacements, generator oil changes, and testing of radios and smoke detectors. In the vehicle, differentiate between an immediate-access bag stowed in the cabin and a larger sustainment cache in the trunk. The immediate-access bag contains everything you need to get yourself or your family through the first short movement: a compact trauma kit, a change of clothing for a child, a couple of liters of water, a power bank, and a basic toolset. The trunk cache can hold heavier, bulkier items, such as additional water, larger medical kits, spare fuel in approved containers, a portable power station, and a more comprehensive tool set. Always be mindful of vehicle ergonomics; heavier items should be positioned lower and closer to the vehicle's center to maintain handling, and critical items must be tethered or secured to prevent them from shifting in a crash or during sudden maneuvers.

Defensive tools other than firearms deserve attention; non-lethal options like chemical deterrents, firm door reinforcement bars, and effective illumination can change the calculus of a confrontation without resorting to lethal force. Where firearms are part of a household's plan, they must be integrated strategically. That integration begins with legality and training: know the laws that govern ownership, storage, transport, and use of force in your jurisdiction, and seek formal instruction that covers safe handling, storage practices, and decision-making under stress. Storage should render weapons inaccessible to unauthorized individuals and should be redundant; for many households, that means a bolted safe or lockbox in the home and a locked container in the vehicle, with separate storage for ammunition if required in your area. Quick-access devices exist, but do not allow perceived convenience to override safe storage practices. Firearms provide a defensive capability unlike any other tool, and when integrated properly, will exponentially increase the ability to defend.

THE STRONGHOLD: HOME AND VEHICLE PREPAREDNESS

Tactics of concealment and visibility are more psychological than technical in nature. In many cases, evidence of preparation can deter opportunists without the need for confrontation. A modest number of visible measures, including lights, a camera, and signs indicating alarm systems, creates uncertainty for someone contemplating an easy score. At the same time, the concentration of obvious defensive indicators, such as large steel gate vaults or overtly tactical vehicles, can attract attention in the wrong context. Many experienced preparers favor blending in, maintaining a normal appearance to reduce curiosity and prevent marking the property as a prize. Simultaneously, the prepared household practices quiet protocols: secure the perimeter at dusk, use routine check-ins with trusted neighbors, and avoid posting detailed absence information on social media that would signal opportunity.

Vehicles impose additional constraints and opportunities for defensive posture. They allow you to carry more, to move faster, and to bridge gaps between hostile points, but they also become targets. Keep visibility and movement under consideration. When staging to depart, position the vehicle so it can leave without complicated maneuvering, ideally backed in with the ability to pull straight out. If you must park on a road, avoid parking in a way that blocks departure, and choose a location that allows for a quick merge onto a main route rather than a slow exit through narrow streets. Understand that choke points in your area, such as bridges, main arterials, and fuel stations, can become dangerous bottlenecks. Plan routes that include alternate options, and keep paper maps in the vehicle in case the GPS becomes unreliable. In extended circumstances or when aiding others, use the vehicle as a relay point. Maintain clear rules about who may ride in or use your vehicle in emergencies; generosity is a moral good, but must be balanced against the safety and sustainment capacity of those under your care.

Good judgment under stress is as trainable as any physical skill. Run drills that exercise the system, such as evening drills where the family moves to the safe room with the lights off, a timed exercise where the vehicle is loaded in the dark, and tabletop discussions that place decision points under simulated pressure. These rehearsals expose friction points, the hard-to-open bag, the missing battery, and the unclear command of roles, and allow you to fix them before they become fatal. After each drill, debrief calmly and update your written procedures. Real events will always have elements of unpredictability; the goal of practice is not to anticipate every variable but to reduce the number of variables you must solve in the moment.

Community remains your greatest multiplier. The household that prepares well but isolates itself misses the advantage of mutual aid. Small, formalized agreements with neighbors, who will check on the elderly, who have a generator with the capacity to charge phones, who can provide shelter for a short period, greatly increase the community's resilience. Share key resources in an organized way: a neighbor who can offer a quiet place to charge devices is different than unplanned offers of shelter from dozens of strangers on the first night after a storm. Cultivate relationships so assistance can be reciprocal and so everyone knows where mutually beneficial resources lie.

There are practical configurations that, when embedded into the home and vehicle, simplify action. Place a waterproof binder and a small secondary power bank in the glove compartment; keep a set of warm clothing folded in a waterproof compression sack beneath the rear seat; store a medical reference card in the binder

THE STRONGHOLD: HOME AND VEHICLE PREPAREDNESS

with concise directions for bleeding control and airway management, accompanied by the names and doses of household medications. In the home, keep a predictable layout: emergency food on a specified shelf labeled with rotation dates, water barrels in a shaded corner with a siphon and a secondary filter nearby, a compact, well-marked medical cabinet with a separate trauma kit accessible from the safe-room. Mount a whiteboard in the command area for situational notes and to record the sequence of events as they happen; this simple habit preserves facts for later legal or insurance processes. Consider redundancies for critical functions: two ways to charge communications, two sources of light in the safe room, multiple channels for weather alerts. The goal is not to hoard but to reduce single points of failure.

Finally, the continuous maintenance of systems matters more than any single acquisition. A generator with stale fuel is worthless; a radio with a dead battery is a broken promise. Maintain a schedule for checks that fits your lifestyle, monthly or quarterly, depending on the item, and keep records of those checks in a small log in your command binder. Replace consumables before they expire, service your vehicle in the seasons when its components are stressed the most, and review your legal knowledge about defensive action annually or when laws change. Habits form the backbone of readiness. The person who checks their vehicle's tire pressure every month, rotates food stores every six months, trains with their firearms regularly, and attends a first-aid refresher annually will be the one whose system holds under pressure.

Preparedness is ultimately an ethic, not a collection of tasks. It is care for family and community expressed through practical action. It requires humility, because no plan is infallible, and generosity, because the aim is to preserve life and to ease suffering wherever possible. The places we frequent, our bodies, our cars, our homes, gain new meaning when we see them as parts of an integrated system. The paramedic, the ambulance, and the hospital do not exist to celebrate the drama of crisis; they exist to preserve life and restore normalcy. Arrange your life the same way. Carry what you need to act, equip your vehicle to extend your reach, and shape your home to be a place of sustainment and refuge. When these components are aligned, you do more than survive; you create the capacity to help others, to restore, and to rebuild.

CHAPTER 8

STRATEGY OF SURVIVAL

The sound of footsteps in the stairwell came first as a small, almost casual rhythm, three light taps, a pause, then another set. Sam heard them through the apartment walls as she was pouring a cup of tea, a mundane domestic motion that suddenly felt out of rhythm with the world. The building was quiet at that hour; most tenants were asleep. She set the kettle down and listened, then listened again. The taps repeated, softer now, as if someone was testing doors. She moved without drama or panic, slow and deliberate to check the peephole. A stranger stood in the corridor, hat on, glancing left and right like someone looking for an opportunity. Sam's training, such as it was, had never been about bravado. She had learned to notice small things: a gait that didn't match purpose, hands tucked away, eyes that avoided contact. She locked the deadbolt, turned off the living room light so the apartment looked dark from the outside, and texted a neighbor a simple phrase they had agreed on for trouble: "All good?" The neighbor replied with a symbol, and in the space of that exchange, Sam made a quiet plan. She would not confront. She would not open the door to curiosity. She moved the baby car seat into the bedroom and closed the baby's room door quietly, then gathered her laptop bag with her wallet, spare keys, handgun, and a compact trauma kit. She placed the bag by the bedroom door and moved to the balcony with a view down the corridor, watching the stranger drift past the door without pausing. When he turned his back, she scooped up the baby carrier, slipped out to the stairwell, and descended two flights to the street, keeping her body close to the rail, moving with purpose and calm. She did not run. She walked briskly, head up, and when a delivery truck rounded the corner, she stepped into its shadow and crossed the sidewalk with steady steps. By the time she reached her car, two neighbors were outside checking on each other. Sam breathed, not because the danger had vanished, but because she had used small, practical measures of awareness, movement, concealment, and community to convert a potential confrontation into a safe exit. That simple, steady choice was the essence of several defensive tactics: escape first, preserve life always, and use the environment, your tools, and your training to turn danger into distance.

Individuals who prepare to defend themselves must begin with a clear, unromantic priority: escape whenever possible. The tactics of confrontation belong second to the imperative of avoiding harm. Yet that does not mean passivity. Defensive tactics in everyday life are a set of principles, habits, and simple maneuvers that increase the probability of avoiding violence or surviving it with the least damage. They are practical, repeatable, and teachable. They combine a mindset, calm, decisive, and morally anchored, with an understanding of movement, environment, and tools. The aim is not to "win" in the prizefight sense but to succeed in the defensive objective you define in advance: escape unharmed, reach a defensible position, or stop an imminent lethal threat when no other option exists. This chapter outlines these principles, including how to move, think, use space, and apply basic physical techniques and tools responsibly and legally. Formal instruction is recommended on every technical topic mentioned here; nothing substitutes for hands-on training with qualified instructors. What follows is a map: principles to practice, concepts to internalize, and actions to rehearse.

The defender's mindset precedes motion. Under stress, decisions become compressed; the body looks for patterns and settles into rehearsed responses. To act usefully in a crisis, you must pre-decide what you value and what you will do to protect it. Decide in advance whether your goal, in any given environment, is to escape, to create distance, to slow an aggressor for an opening, or to stop lethal force. Those goals require different tactics. Escape requires creating angles and opportunities to move away; delaying an attacker requires barriers and noise to buy time; stopping deadly force requires decisive intervention by capable individuals. Train the mind to accept that escape is the preferred outcome, and rehearse those escape options until the body can execute them without indecision.

Movement is your most reliable tool. People under threat often freeze, not because they lack will, but because their bodies default to unpracticed behavior. The solution is simple repetition of basic motion and repositioning drills. Practice turning while moving, stepping off linear paths, and changing your rhythm as you walk. A straight line is predictable; an angled exit is harder to anticipate and intercept. A fundamental concept here is the idea of presenting moving targets; the human body is less vulnerable when in motion. Keep your hands free if possible; if you must carry items, organize them into a grab-and-go bag that does not impede mobility. In crowded spaces, use the flow of people to shield your movement, move with groups when it's safe, and utilize the periphery when you need to break away. Recognize choke points: narrow corridors, single exits, and stairwells are areas that concentrate risk. Whenever possible, avoid them or plan your exit through them with a secondary option in mind.

Angles are the language of spatial advantage. A "winning angle" is any position that offers you greater control of the engagement's geometry, offering you the ability to move, to see more of the environment, and to limit the adversary's options. Winning angles are not about aggression; they are about survival. Consider a simple example: if someone approaches you from your right on a sidewalk and you step diagonally left and forward, you move onto an angle that places visual and temporal advantage in your favor; the aggressor must change direction and speed, losing their intended timeline. The diagonal step is the smallest tactical act, but its effect is outsized. Winning angles serve three core functions: they create space between you and the threat, they expose or deny options for the adversary, and they position you relative to escape routes or cover. Learn to read the environment for these angles, including doorways positioned at oblique degrees, parked vehicles that can provide concealment, cover, and space, and stairwells that allow you to change your vertical position and rehearse movement to them until it becomes instinctive.

Positioning is the practical application of angles. In any confrontation, seek a location that gives you multiple options: the ability to move, the ability to call for help, and the ability to use barriers between you and a threat. A defensible position need not be a fortress. A hallway with multiple exits, a table that creates a physical barrier, or a raised curb that slows pursuit are all practical advantages. Avoid positions that trap you against a wall with no escape. Use lighting to your advantage; good illumination reveals intent and reduces the chance of surprise. Conversely, if concealment serves your escape, use shadows and obstacles mindfully, but do so with the priority of moving to a place where you can then call for assistance.

Use the environment as a force multiplier. A common error is treating tools and skills in isolation. The most attainable advantage in any defensive incident is the integrated use of environment, tool, and skill. For example, pulling a table or chair between you and an intruder is not elegant, but it creates a barrier that buys time and complicates the attacker's approach. A car door used as cover while moving to the driver's seat is not an offensive maneuver; it is a practical step to regain mobility. Everyday objects can be used to delay or distract: dropping a heavy bag to the floor can momentarily obstruct the path; tipping a table toward a threat complicates their path. The point is not to glamorize improvised barriers but to recognize that the environment is always present and that creative, pragmatic use of it often changes outcomes more reliably than unpracticed strikes.

Voice and communication are tools with disproportionate power. A loud, clear command such as "Back away!" or "Stop!" projects focus and can disrupt an assailant's plan because most opportunistic attackers rely on surprise and uncertainty. Use a deliberate, controlled tone. Panic screams rarely help; clear commands establish authority and may attract attention. If you cannot safely use your voice, consider prearranged signals with companions or neighbors, texts, discrete clicks, or a known phrase that prompts immediate support. Remember that calling 911 or local emergency services is not an admission of weakness; it is a decisive act. Provide concise information: location, number of assailants, weapons observed, and your immediate needs. If in public, point to witnesses and instruct them to call for help. The social presence of third parties dramatically reduces the likelihood of escalation in some cases.

When escape is impossible and confrontation becomes inevitable, the principles of eliciting advantage shift from movement to disruption. The goal remains the same: to preserve life, but the measures may become kinetic. In such circumstances, aim to create an immediate opportunity to escape or to disable the threat long enough for you to flee. Target selection matters: aim for simple, gross-motor targets that cause pain or disruption without requiring fine aim. Eyes, nose, jaw, neck, and groin are functional targets because strikes there invoke immediate motor responses and can create openings. The value is not in precision but in the capacity to disrupt an attacker's balance, breathing, or will to continue. Train in basic, repeatable strikes, palm strikes, heel-of-hand, elbow drives, and knee strikes that require little space to execute and can be performed under stress. Avoid complex techniques that require fine motor control when adrenaline constricts dexterity.

Close-quarters grappling awareness is another relevant skill. Many real assaults involve clinch proximity, where large, powerful weapons are not at play, but leverage and control determine outcomes. Learn simple escapes from commonly used holds: break the wrist grip by turning the thumb toward the weak point while stepping off-line, use your hips to create separation in clinches, and remember that the shortest path to freedom is often an explosive step sideways rather than a direct push. A ground strategy should be conservative for individuals; avoid going to the ground unless you have no alternative, as it often exposes you to additional threats and makes mobility difficult. If forced to the ground, protect your airway, control distance with your legs where possible, and create opportunities to regain your feet by shuffling to your side and using frames to push.

STRATEGY OF SURVIVAL

Decision-making under stress, the cognitive dimension of tactics, is as trainable as striking. Mental rehearsals, visualization, and scenario-based practice build the neural pathways you need when consciousness narrows. Run through scenarios in your mind: a stranger following you, a vehicle blocking your path, a sudden shove in a crowded bar. Ask yourself, beforehand, what you will do: turn into a lighted storefront, step toward a group, use the car as a barrier, or call out a neighbor's name for help. Mental rehearsals should be specific and sensory-rich. Imagine the feel of the sidewalk, the sound of footsteps, and the weight of the bag so that under stress, the brain recognizes the pattern and moves to rehearsed solutions.

Tools, as discussed earlier, play a crucial role in solving the puzzle. Nonlethal and lawful options like personal alarms, bright flashlights, pepper spray, tasers, where legal, and compact trauma kits fit most plans and lifestyles. Choose tools you can deploy quickly and that do not create additional legal or practical liabilities. A personal alarm can disorient and attract attention; a high-lumen flashlight can temporarily blind and create an opening to flee. If pepper spray is legal where you live and you choose to carry it, practice deploying it safely and understand the risks associated with wind, crowd, and secondary exposure. Whatever tool you carry, integrate it into drills so that deployment under stress is smooth. Remember that tools are force multipliers, not substitutes for awareness or movement.

Firearms elevate both capability and responsibility. They are not an option for everyone and, where chosen, must be incorporated with rigorous training, secure storage, and legal knowledge. A firearm is a last-resort instrument to stop an imminent lethal threat. The decision to use it carries permanent ethical, legal, and psychological consequences. If you elect to own firearms, invest in professional instruction that emphasizes not only marksmanship but judgment, de-escalation, and post-incident procedure. Train in scenario-based contexts, force-on-force simulation, and stress inoculation to ensure that the user can make clear decisions under pressure. Integrate firearms training with medical preparedness. If a shooting occurs, blood loss may be the immediate threat to life, and your ability to apply tourniquets and maintain safety for victims and responders becomes critical. Store firearms securely and have protocols for access that prevent unauthorized use by children or guests. Review laws on the use of force in your jurisdiction and consult counsel when in doubt. Firearms can preserve life, but without discipline and legal awareness, they can produce tragedy.

Strategic thinking also turns on time management. Calculate the time you need to escape, the time it takes for responders to arrive, and the time you can sustain a defensive posture. Create friction that buys time for help: lock doors, create obstacles, shout for witnesses, and move to positions where you can control sightlines and exit options - every second matters. Use timers in training to measure how long it takes to perform critical tasks like retrieving a bag, locking a door, deploying a firearm, or dialing emergency services, and then practice until those times decrease reliably.

After-action matters as much as action. Surviving an incident does not end the job; it is just the beginning. Secure the scene if safe to do so: preserve evidence, avoid contaminating the area, and document details as soon as possible. Seek medical evaluation even if injuries seem minor; adrenaline masks pain, and internal injuries can be insidious. Recognize that trauma carries psychological effects; arrange for counseling and legal guidance promptly. Prepare a statement of events to share with law enforcement that

STRATEGY OF SURVIVAL

is factual and concise, avoiding conjecture. This post-incident discipline helps preserve your legal position and facilitates recovery.

Training is the bridge between principle and performance. Attend classes that teach situational awareness, escape techniques, verbal de-escalation, basic striking, and trauma care. Prefer instructors who emphasize civilian needs over competitive sports or military aggression; look for courses that include stress inoculation, scenario-based drills, and legal discussion. Partner training with a trusted companion builds coordinated responses: practicing silent signals, escape routes, and rendezvous points lets two people act as a unit rather than independent actors in panic. Regularity matters - skills degrade without repetition. A realistic training cadence might be short, frequent refreshers combined with periodic immersive simulations.

Practice humility in all planning. The overconfident defender takes unnecessary risks. Measure your capabilities honestly and design tactics that match your strengths. If you are not physically strong, exploit distance, angles, and tools. If you are fast, rehearse sprint and transition drills. The point is to leverage who you are and what skills you possess and build your skillset to be as well-rounded as possible.

Finally, embed tactics in the community. A prepared person is not isolated; they are part of a neighborhood system where awareness and mutual support multiply safety. Share plans discreetly with trusted neighbors. Establish simple protocols for checking on each other during unusual hours. The presence of a few prepared people in a block reduces the likelihood of targeted aggression because predators seek low-friction, low attention targets. Offer to teach basic skills or to organize community training for first aid, safe movement, and defensive action. The collective benefit is enormous.

Defensive tactics for individuals are not an arsenal of combative arts but a mature doctrine of survival: escape, preserve, and, when unavoidable, stop threats in a manner that aligns with law and conscience. Win by choosing the outcome that protects life. Sometimes winning is placing distance between yourself and danger, sometimes it is using the environment to delay and call for help, and in the worst-case scenarios, it is to stop lethal force with decisive, legally justifiable action. Practice each part of this doctrine until the body and mind can execute it without debate.

The last, quiet layer of this work is the cultivation of moral clarity and calm. Defensive skill without ethics is dangerous. Train to act with restraint and purpose. Teach children and companions not to emulate aggression but to prioritize safety and reporting. Reflect often on what it means to defend life, not to glorify violence, but to prevent it from destroying the people you love. That reflection guides how you learn, what you carry, and how you behave under pressure.

There is no perfect plan and no guaranteed outcome, only preparation that stacks the odds in your favor. The everyday tactics and strategy of an individual defender are simple in concept and profound in effect: notice more, step away early, use angles and cover, carry practical tools, practice physical responses, seek instruction, and sustain a mindset of calm purpose. Preventive motion is the highest victory; when motion is impossible, decisive action coupled with a plan to regain safety is the next. When the crisis is over, the discipline continues: medical care, documentation, emotional processing, and legal clarity. Live with that rhythm. Rehearse, refine, and share what you learn. The best defense is rarely flashy or violent. It is quiet, prepared, and humane. It preserves life and returns you, intact, to the ordinary business of being alive.

CHAPTER 9

THE AFTERMATH

It was one of those winter evenings where the cold seemed to have a presence of its own, pressing against the windows and crawling under the cracks of the doors. The snow had started sometime in the afternoon, a lazy drift that turned the streets quiet and coated everything in soft, unbroken white. By the time Josh pulled into his driveway, the sky had gone dark, and the neighborhood looked frozen in stillness. He liked nights like that: peaceful and predictable. He worked long hours as an electrician and had learned to savor the few hours of solitude that came after the day was done. The house was empty that night; his wife was visiting her parents a few towns over, and his teenage son was at a friend's house. It was rare for the place to be this quiet.

Josh moved through his usual routine, the rhythm of habit offering comfort. He set his boots by the door, poured himself a nice tall glass of cranberry juice, and sat down at the small table near the window where he could watch the snow fall in the amber glow of the streetlight. There was a kind of peace in that stillness, the sort of moment that makes you forget the weight of everything else. When he finally turned off the TV and headed toward his bedroom, it was nearly midnight. He checked the locks, as he always did, and felt that quiet reassurance of safety settle over him.

He was half asleep when the first sound reached him. It wasn't loud, just a soft metallic clatter, the kind of sound a house sometimes makes when the temperature drops. He rolled onto his side and waited, telling himself it was nothing. Then came another sound, a lot closer this time. A scrape against the back door. A pause. Then the muffled thud of something heavy hitting the porch.

He was fully awake now. For a moment, he stayed still, listening. His heartbeat filled his ears, and the room felt suddenly smaller. Then came the unmistakable sound of the doorknob twisting, slow and deliberate. The old brass fixture rattled once, then again, followed by the hollow creak of the frame giving way.

He slid out of bed and reached for the small safe bolted nearby. His hands felt colder than they should have been. The combination came easily, practiced. He opened it, took out his handgun, and grabbed the flashlight. From the hallway came the faint shuffle of feet on the hardwood floor. Whoever it was had made it inside.

Josh moved toward the doorway, staying low. His mind was a blur of fragments, his wife's voice reminding him to lock the windows, the safety instructor's calm repetition of "identify, decide, act," the echo of every news story he'd ever read about home invasions that ended badly. When the intruder stepped into view, the man was silhouetted by the faint streetlight bleeding through the curtains. A heavy coat, hood pulled low, a crowbar in one hand, and the glint of something metallic in the other.

Josh didn't speak at first. The words wouldn't come. His throat felt dry. The man moved forward, his breath visible in the cold air that spilled through the open door behind him. That was when instinct and training took over. "Stop," Josh said, his voice low but steady. "Don't move."

The man froze for a second, then took another step forward. There was no plea, no hesitation, just the sudden, violent movement of the arm rising, the shine of metal cutting through the dim light. The next moments were fragmented, unreal. Josh saw his own hands extend, felt the recoil but not the sound. The flash lit the hallway for an instant, and then the intruder was on the floor, motionless. The sounds and bits of silence that followed were unbearable.

For a long time, Josh didn't move. The air smelled of gunpowder and cold. His breath came in ragged bursts, and the house seemed impossibly large around him. The gun was still in his hands, his finger stiff against the frame. When he finally lowered it, his hands were trembling. He found his phone and dialed 911, his voice flat, almost detached. "There's been a break-in. I had to shoot him." The words didn't sound real, even to him.

When the flashing lights finally filled the street, the scene outside looked surreal. Snowflakes drifted lazily through the beams, melting on the officers' jackets as they shouted commands. Josh did everything he'd trained himself to do; he followed directives, stepped back, and raised his hands high. The officers moved fast, weapons drawn, eyes wide with adrenaline. They cuffed him before they asked a single question. The cold metal bit into his wrists, grounding him in the reality that his life had just changed forever.

He sat in the back of the squad car, the heater blasting, watching his own breath fog the window. He could hear the radio chatter and see the silhouettes of paramedics moving inside his house, as well as the flicker of camera flashes as investigators documented everything. The snow kept falling, soft and indifferent, erasing the footprints that led up to his door.

At the station, the hours blurred together. Questions came in waves, some sharp, some quiet, all heavy with implication. The detectives weren't cruel, but they weren't kind either. They asked why he hadn't stayed in the bedroom, why he hadn't called sooner, and whether he'd given any warning before shooting. Every answer felt like stepping deeper into quicksand. He knew he'd done what he had to do, but explaining it out loud made it sound like something else, something deliberate, something planned. He could feel the weight of every word. When his lawyer finally arrived, Josh stopped talking. The silence that followed was almost a relief.

In the days that came after, the house didn't feel like his anymore. The broken door was repaired, but the cold still seemed to linger there, creeping under the threshold like a reminder. The neighbors looked at him differently. Some nodded with quiet sympathy; others avoided his eyes altogether. The local news had run a short piece about the shooting, just enough to make the rounds on social media. Half the comments praised him for protecting his home. The other half called him a killer.

The investigation dragged on. There were interviews, depositions, statements, and the slow grind of the legal machinery, which had no interest in the emotions attached to it. Josh learned quickly that being justified in your actions didn't mean being free from scrutiny. He wasn't the hero of his own story anymore. He was evidence, testimony, and paperwork. He was a case number.

The prosecutor eventually declined to file charges, but the relief he expected never came. The man he shot had a record of theft, assault, and drug use, and the facts of the case were clear.

However, clarity doesn't always make you sleep better at night. It doesn't stop the sound from replaying in your head when the house goes quiet. He found himself avoiding certain parts of the hallway, unable to look at the spot where the man had fallen. He replayed the scene in his mind, searching for the moment when something else might have changed the outcome. It never did.

The civil suit came months later, filed by the intruder's family. They claimed excessive force, wrongful death, and negligence. It didn't matter that the man had been armed or that he'd forced his way in. Civil court doesn't work on guilt; it works on liability and seemingly sympathy. The process was long, invasive, and exhausting. The lawyers dissected his finances, his training, his social media posts, even the way he described firearms in casual conversations. He sat through depositions where every choice he'd made that night was picked apart by people who had never felt the chill of fear crawl up their spine.

The settlement came eventually, smaller than the plaintiff had wanted but still enough to leave a mark. Between legal fees, lost work time, and the cost of repairs, Josh's savings were gone. He sold a few tools and canceled a vacation he and his wife had planned. The stress wore on them both. There were arguments, mostly about things that weren't really about anything, about how the house felt different, about the quiet, about the way he avoided specific conversations. They worked through it, slowly, but the life they returned to wasn't the same one they'd left behind that night.

When the shooting stops, the longest battle begins.

The aftermath of a defensive encounter is rarely clean. It is a process, a maze of legal, emotional, and financial trials that can overwhelm even the most composed person. Many people train for the moment itself, the confrontation, the mechanics of

THE AFTERMATH

shooting, and the split-second decision-making required to save their lives. Far fewer prepare for what follows, for the weeks and months where adrenaline fades and bureaucracy takes over. That is where most people are caught unprepared.

The first reality to understand is that after any defensive shooting, you are no longer in control. Once the police arrive, the event no longer belongs to you; it belongs to the system. The responding officers are not there to comfort or congratulate you. Their first priority is to secure the scene, identify threats, and preserve evidence. That means you, too, are part of the investigation. It isn't easy to accept, but it's essential to understand. You will be treated as a potential suspect because, from their perspective, that's precisely what you are until the evidence tells them otherwise.

The initial encounter with law enforcement can set the tone for everything that follows. Adrenaline, confusion, and exhaustion will make clear thinking nearly impossible. That's why preparation before an incident is so vital. Knowing what to do in those moments - how to communicate, how to compose yourself, and what not to say can make the difference between clarity and chaos. The goal is not to talk your way out of trouble. The goal is to survive the process without exacerbating the situation. That means following commands completely, keeping your hands visible, identifying yourself as the victim, pointing out evidence and witnesses if you can, and then remaining silent until you have legal representation.

In the hours after a shooting, your body and mind will not always be fully reliable sources of information. Your perception will have been distorted by stress, and your memory will be fragmented by adrenaline. It is normal to misremember small details or to struggle to piece together the sequence of events. That isn't deception, it's physiology. However, to investigators, inconsistencies can look like dishonesty. That is why having legal counsel present before giving a full statement is essential. A trained attorney understands both the law and the effects of stress, and they can help ensure that what you say reflects the truth without being twisted by misunderstanding or emotion.

Once the initial investigation begins, patience becomes your greatest ally. The system moves slowly. Evidence must be processed, reports written, and prosecutors must review the findings. During that time, you may feel powerless, exposed, and uncertain of your future. It is easy to second-guess yourself, to replay every choice and wonder if you could have done something different. That doubt is natural, but it cannot change what's already done. The truth is that even a completely justified act of self-defense can lead to arrest, charges, or months of legal scrutiny. The law recognizes the right to defend oneself, but it also demands accountability for every trigger pull.

If criminal charges do arise, the process becomes a test of endurance. Court dates, hearings, and media attention can weigh heavily on individuals. Prosecutors may attempt to portray your actions as reckless or unnecessary. The emotional toll of sitting in a courtroom while your character and decisions are dissected can be immense. This is why legal representation is not optional; it is a matter of survival. A qualified defense attorney will ensure the facts are presented clearly and that your rights are protected from the moment the investigation begins.

Even if the criminal case is resolved in your favor, there is often another battle waiting: the civil lawsuit. The family of the attacker, regardless of circumstances, may sue for wrongful death or injury. Civil law operates under a lower standard of proof, meaning the scales don't have to tip far to make life difficult. These lawsuits can stretch for years, draining finances and patience. Legal defense funds or concealed carry insurance are not luxuries; they are necessities. They provide access to lawyers, expert witnesses, and financial support when everything else seems uncertain.

Beyond the courtroom lies another kind of aftermath, the one that unfolds inside. The emotional and psychological weight of taking a life, even in defense, can be heavy. Many find themselves haunted by flashes of the event, by the sound, the image, the what-ifs. Some feel guilt even when none is warranted. Others feel anger at how quickly they became the focus of suspicion rather than sympathy. This is a normal human response to trauma. It is the mind trying to make sense of violence. It is also the part of the process that no amount of tactical training can prepare you for.

Recovery requires more than time. It requires awareness, honesty, and sometimes professional help. Post-traumatic stress doesn't belong only to soldiers. It belongs to anyone who has faced imminent danger and survived it. Counseling can help sort through those emotions, teach coping mechanisms, and prevent the slow erosion that comes from unresolved trauma. Talking about it with someone who understands the psychology of critical incidents is not a sign of weakness; it's an act of responsibility.

Family dynamics often shift in the wake of a defensive incident. Loved ones may struggle to understand the emotional distance or the restlessness that follows. Children might ask questions that are difficult to answer. Spouses might carry their own anxiety, wondering what would have happened if they'd been there. These conversations require patience. Open communication about fear, doubt, and recovery is vital. Bottling it up creates distance, and distance can quietly destroy what the incident itself could not.

Preparation for the aftermath must also include practical planning. That means securing your home against tampering after an investigation, maintaining clear records of firearm training, understanding where your weapon will be stored as evidence, and knowing how to handle the media if approached. It also means preparing for the financial consequences, like bail, legal fees, time off work, and potential relocation. Few people anticipate how far the ripple effect spreads; those who do tend to weather it better.

Perhaps the most overlooked part of preparation is the mindset of restraint. Carrying a weapon changes how you move through the world, and it must also change how you think. Every confrontation carries the potential for lifelong consequences. Knowing when not to draw, when to retreat, and when to de-escalate are the marks of maturity, not fear. Self-defense begins with awareness, but it ends with judgment. The most successful defenders are those who recognize that the ultimate goal is to win, but do so through that avenue that brings the least potential for consequences when possible.

The aftermath of deadly force is not about glory or vindication. It is about survival in every sense, physical, legal, emotional, and moral. It is about learning that the act of defending your life does not shield you from pain, loss, or consequence. However, it can be faced with preparation, with knowledge, and with humility. The time to prepare is long before that winter night ever arrives, before the snow falls, before the silence breaks, before the decision is forced upon you. This is because when that moment comes, the only thing more important than surviving it is being ready to survive everything that follows.

CHAPTER 10

THE DEFENDER'S DISCIPLINE

It was still dark when Nick's alarm went off. He didn't hit snooze. He never did. The small digital clock on his nightstand blinked 4:45am, and the sound of winter wind against the window hinted at how cold the morning would be. Still, he swung his legs over the edge of the bed, stretched his shoulders, and sat there for a moment, letting his mind wake before his body followed. Mornings were his foundation, the time of day when no one asked anything of him, when the world was still quiet enough to think clearly.

His routine had been built slowly over many years, adjusted and refined, never perfect but always deliberate. He wasn't training for competition or trying to prove anything to anyone. He trained for the same reason he carried a firearm and lived with awareness: because life was unpredictable, and preparation wasn't a phase; it was a way of living.

He started every morning the same way, with breath work. Three slow inhales, three measured exhales, clearing the fog of sleep and setting his mind. Some mornings, he meditated for ten minutes, some days only two. It wasn't about perfection; it was about discipline. He'd learned that stillness was as crucial as movement. Awareness didn't begin with seeing the world outside; it began with understanding the world inside.

By five, he was in the garage gym. Nothing fancy, just a squat rack, a pull-up bar, a few kettlebells, and a heavy bag that had seen better years. He didn't chase numbers anymore. Strength, endurance, mobility, and recovery were his focus. The training was functional, from deadlifts to pushups, rows, carries, and sprints. Enough to keep his body capable, because he'd long since learned that physical capability was the backbone of every other skill. The stronger his body, the steadier his mind.

After training, he made breakfast, packed his gear, and headed out. His concealed carry routine was quiet and methodical; firearm checked, spare magazine seated, belt adjusted. He didn't think of it as gearing up for danger, but as maintaining readiness. Like brushing teeth or locking doors, it was a habit, and habits, he believed, were the armor of preparedness.

Nick worked as a construction manager, often moving between sites, neighborhoods, and crews. He didn't walk through life paranoid, but he was observant. He made a game of reading his environment, watching traffic flow, identifying exits, and noting body language in crowds. It wasn't about suspicion; it was about awareness. Situational awareness wasn't constant tension. It was quiet mindfulness, a balanced alertness that became second nature.

At lunch, he ate simple meals, nothing extreme, just enough to keep his energy even. In the evenings, he alternated between range practice, dry fire, or skill work. Sometimes that meant drawing from concealment and firing a single precise shot.

Sometimes it meant running movement drills at the range or practicing low-light techniques. More often than not, though, it was dry fire at home, simple repetitions in front of a mirror, focusing on economy of motion and a clean trigger press. He logged every session. Not because anyone asked him to, but because accountability kept him honest.

Once a week, he met with a small group of like-minded friends to train scenario-based drills. They didn't just shoot; they talked through decisions, reactions, and communication. One of them played the "bad guy," another acted as a witness, and they ran through how to give clear commands, move to cover, or handle post-incident behavior. They learned not just how to shoot, but how to think.

Nick's weekends were for recovery and reflection. He hiked, spent time with his family, read about case studies and defensive encounters, and made time for silence. He knew that overtraining or obsessing could be as dangerous as apathy. His training was sustainable because it was balanced. He maintained strength, skill, and awareness without sacrificing peace. He understood the simple truth: preparation wasn't about living in fear; it was about earning the right to live in peace.

That kind of balance doesn't happen by accident. It's built brick by brick, day by day, through habits that reinforce discipline without burning out the mind or body. Nick's example isn't extraordinary. It's practical, attainable, and repeatable. Anyone can live this way, with structure, consistency, and perspective. What separates the prepared from the unprepared isn't luck or money; it's the willingness to build and maintain a lifestyle that supports readiness without becoming consumed by it.

The process begins with mindset. Every skill in defensive living, whether awareness, marksmanship, or physical fitness, depends on mental clarity and discipline. You cannot train effectively if you do not first train the mind that drives the body. Awareness starts in small, everyday moments. It is not about suspicion or paranoia but observation. Each day, you can refine this skill in ordinary ways: noting exits when you enter a restaurant, observing where people congregate, paying attention to who seems out of place or agitated, and simply asking yourself what you would do if something unexpected happened. The brain learns through repetition, and over time, these observations become automatic, freeing you to act decisively instead of reactively.

Daily awareness training doesn't require danger; it demands attention. When driving, avoid being lost in thought. When walking, lift your eyes from your phone. When pumping gas, stand facing outward, not inward. These small choices compound. They teach your brain to maintain an active picture of your environment, known in some circles as situational comprehension. This ability is perishable, just like marksmanship. If you stop practicing it, you drift back into complacency.

Physical readiness is another pillar. The body is the vehicle through which all action must pass. If it is weak, slow, or neglected, even the sharpest mind will be trapped by its limitations. Strength, endurance, and mobility form the foundation of self-defense. You do not need to be a professional athlete, but you must be capable. A body that can sprint, lift, fight, and recover is a body that can survive.

A sustainable physical training routine focuses on balance. Train your strength with resistance exercises, such as bodyweight exercises, free weights, or resistance bands. Train endurance through cardio like running, cycling, swimming, or interval training. Train mobility with stretching or yoga to prevent injury. These disciplines reinforce each other. The goal is not specialization but versatility. Each session doesn't need to be long; it needs to be consistent. Maintaining a few sessions each week, over the course of years, will accomplish more than sporadic bursts of intensity followed by long periods of inactivity.

Mental health ties directly to performance. Stress, fatigue, and anxiety dull reaction time and cloud judgment. The defender's mind must be calm even in chaos. This isn't natural; it is trained. Mindfulness exercises, controlled breathing, and short moments of meditation teach emotional regulation. They allow the mind to slow down in a crisis and the body to obey commands under stress. A prepared mind is not fearless; it is functional under fear.

Proficiency, especially with firearms, requires a structured approach. Shooting, like any defensive subject, is a perishable skill; without repetition, it decays. Daily dry fire practice builds muscle memory and trigger discipline. Weekly or biweekly live fire confirms those skills under recoil. Monthly drills should test a mix of fundamentals and dynamic movement: drawing from concealment, reloading under pressure, engaging from cover, and shooting in varied light. Every few months, evaluate accuracy and speed metrics, track group sizes, shot times, and consistency to ensure optimal performance. The numbers don't define you, but they reveal progress or decay.

Equally important are the soft skills, namely verbal commands, de-escalation, and communication under pressure. These can be practiced with a partner or even alone. Rehearse issuing firm, clear instructions like "Stay back!" or "Drop the weapon!" with proper projection and tone. Record yourself, listen, and refine your work. Confidence in your voice can often prevent violence entirely. Decision-making under stress can be trained through mental rehearsals. Visualize scenarios such as parking lots, hallways, and traffic jams, then think through your options. The more often you mentally walk through these decisions, the faster your mind will recognize patterns in reality.

Defensive preparation extends beyond the range or gym. Every home should have a plan. Walk through your house with intention. Identify safe rooms, fields of fire, and points of cover. Practice moving family members to safety, calling for help, and communicating under stress. Review and adjust as the environment changes with new furniture, new locks, and new routines. Just as fire drills prepare for disaster, self-defense rehearsals prepare for crisis. They build calm through familiarity.

Weekly habits can sustain awareness and skill without becoming overwhelming. Set aside time to review news stories or case studies about defensive incidents. Analyze what went right and what went wrong. Study not only the tactics but the decision-making, the aftermath, and the mistakes. Experience is the most brutal teacher; learning from others allows you to absorb lessons without having to pay the price yourself.

Monthly, dedicate time to reassess your equipment and mindset. Check that your firearm is maintained and functions perfectly, that your holster is comfortable, safe, and properly adjusted, that your ammunition is fresh enough and free from defect, and that your emergency contacts and legal preparations are current. Review your training logs. Reflect on whether you've grown complacent in any area, such as your awareness, fitness, or skill. Adjust accordingly. Preparation is not static; it's a cycle. Each month should close with an honest look at where you stand and what needs improvement.

Annually, conduct a full readiness audit. Take a professional class utilizing firearms, combatives, medical, or situational response. Skills learned under supervision evolve faster and correct bad habits that personal repetition can entrench. Attend a force-on-force course to experience stress inoculation. Practice with others, exchange ideas, and renew your understanding. Growth stagnates in isolation; the presence of other dedicated learners raises the standard.

Beyond physical and technical readiness, community matters. Surround yourself with people who share values of responsibility, discipline, and respect. Training partners hold you accountable, provide motivation, and offer perspectives you might miss. Shared purpose builds resilience. It prevents burnout and sustains enthusiasm through years of training.

Preparedness is a lifelong pursuit, not a destination. The defender's journey is cyclical- learning, refining, maintaining, and adapting. Skills degrade if ignored. Awareness dulls without use. Fitness fades without effort. Even the most resilient mindset requires renewal, lest fear and complacency creep in. The key is sustainability. Training should fit life, not overwhelm it. Balance intensity with recovery, seriousness with joy, vigilance with peace. You cannot live well if you live only for crises.

Consistency matters more than perfection. Five minutes of daily awareness practice, ten minutes of dry fire, three short workouts per week, and a monthly reflection can transform a person over time. The transformation happens quietly and habit stacking until preparedness becomes identity. The goal isn't to chase extremes; it's to build a rhythm that lasts decades.

Preparedness also demands humility. There is no final mastery. Every skill can erode, every plan can fail, every person can falter under pressure. Training is not a guarantee against fear or failure; it is reinforcement against helplessness. You train partially to control the outcome, but primarily to increase your odds of surviving whatever comes. That's why the work never ends. The habits you form today will determine how you respond years from now when everything depends on them.

Actual readiness is quiet. It doesn't draw attention, doesn't boast. It's the calm confidence that comes from knowing you've done the work. It's the steady awareness of your surroundings without paranoia, the strength to move decisively without hesitation, and the humility to keep learning because you understand how fragile control really is.

In the end, a well-rounded training regimen isn't about weapons or drills or checklists; it's about living deliberately and habitually. It's about refusing to coast through life unprepared for its unpredictable turns. It's about investing time and energy into building habits that protect what matters most: life, family, peace of mind. Since the goal of all this training, awareness, and discipline isn't to live in fear of danger, it's to earn the freedom to live without it controlling you.

The person who trains consistently, who tends to their body, sharpens their mind, and maintains awareness, is not living in tension; they're living in strength. Every repetition, every observation, every breath taken with intention is a deposit into the account of survival and peace. When the day comes that they need to draw upon it, whether it's to act, to endure, or simply to stay calm, they won't be searching for strength. They'll already have it.

Skills fade. Awareness dulls. Strength wanes. However, the discipline to maintain them, the humility to keep learning, and the perseverance to stay consistent are the mark of someone truly prepared, because survival, in the end, belongs not to the strongest or the fastest, but to the most practiced, the most aware, and the most willing to keep showing up long after everyone else stops.

Now, that is the quiet truth of readiness. It's not dramatic, it's not cinematic, and it's not fleeting. It's the slow, steady grind of preparation built day by day, decision by decision, until it becomes indistinguishable from who you are.

CHAPTER 11

ENDURING READINESS

There comes a point in the journey of preparation when drilling becomes routine, the lessons compound, and what remains is not just a collection of skills, but a way of living. The defender's path is not defined by confrontation; it's defined by care, by the deep and quiet love for the lives that depend on your courage, your calm, and your choices. It's not a life built around fear, but one that honors peace by being ready to preserve it. That readiness, when shaped by love, becomes something more than defense. It becomes stewardship. It becomes a way of moving through the world with purpose, awareness, and responsibility.

From the beginning, this journey has never been about learning to fight. It has always been about learning to live, to live awake, disciplined, and grounded in a moral compass that doesn't waver when tested. The loving defender understands that the duty to protect is not a license for pride or dominance; it is a calling to humility and vigilance. Every act of preparation, every moment of awareness, every repetition at the range or in the gym is not an act of aggression; it's an act of service. It's a declaration that life is worth defending, and that peace is worth preserving through discipline and restraint.

The person who walks this path knows that proper defensive capability begins long before the moment of danger. It starts in the quiet decisions that no one sees. It continues in how you speak to others, how you manage your emotions, and how you walk through a room without needing to control it. The loving defender cultivates calm. They understand that conflict avoided is victory multiplied. They train not just for what they might need to do, but for who they must become if that moment ever arrives. The readiness to act and the discipline to hold back are two sides of the same coin, and both are earned through self-awareness and practice.

Living the life of a loving defender means realizing that strength without compassion is incomplete. To carry the ability to take a life while choosing daily to preserve it is one of the most incredible acts of self-control a person can practice. This is the essence of maturity in defensive capability, not the desire to fight, but the commitment to protect; not the pursuit of power, but the stewardship of peace. This mindset separates the reckless from the responsible, the armed from the prepared, the overly aggressive from the controlled and capable.

Preparation has always been more about the heart than the hand. The skills, drills, and routines are expressions of intent, but they are not the source of it. The source lies in the love that anchors it all: love for family, love for freedom, and love for life itself. The loving defender trains so that fear cannot rule, so that chaos cannot destroy, and so that they can face the unknown without trembling. When that love drives preparation, every repetition gains meaning. Every act of discipline becomes sacred.

There will always be those who misunderstand this way of life. They will see readiness and assume paranoia. They will see skill and assume violence. However, the truth is that the loving defender is often the gentlest person in the room. They don't walk in anger, and they don't look for trouble. Their calm is not the stillness of ignorance, but the peace that comes from knowing they have done the work. They understand that violence is not a desire, but a duty that may one day fall upon them. In preparing for that burden, they remove its power to define them.

The awareness that runs through this life is quiet but constant. It isn't a state of fear; it's a state of respect. Respect for how fragile life is, how unpredictable the world can be, and how quickly peace can shatter when carelessness replaces vigilance. To live aware is to walk with eyes open and ego subdued. It is to see the patterns others ignore, the open door, the distracted stranger, the uneasy energy in a room, not just living on the edge, but to live engaged. Awareness is love translated into attention. When you are truly present, you protect more than yourself; you safeguard everyone within your reach.

Physical readiness matters too, but not for vanity or bravado. The defender's body is not sculpted for appearance; it is conditioned for service. It must be strong enough to endure, flexible enough to adapt, and resilient enough to recover. Strength supports restraint. The body becomes a tool for stability, not destruction. Every rep, every run, every bead of sweat is a rehearsal for the day when your body may be the only barrier between chaos and those you love. Physical training, when guided by purpose, becomes a form of gratitude, a way of saying thank you for the gift of health, and of ensuring you can stand when others cannot.

The mind, too, must be kept in readiness. The defender's mind is the command center of all else, the seat of judgment, clarity, and courage. Training the mind means learning to think through fear rather than being consumed by it. It means practicing decision-making in moments of calm so that you can make swift decisions in moments of crisis. It means studying not only tactics but your belief system, understanding that the difference between justified and reckless is often a matter of one second's thought. The loving defender never stops learning, because knowledge is the shield that protects both the innocent and the conscience.

Discipline, above all, is what holds the pieces together. Without discipline, awareness fades, skills deteriorate, and fitness declines. Discipline is the bridge between intention and reality. It is the quiet voice that says, "Do it anyway," on days when you don't feel like training, practicing, or thinking. The loving defender knows that discipline isn't about punishment but consistency. It's how we ensure that our actions will align with our values when life tests us most.

Responsibility is the core of this life. To take ownership of your safety and that of others is not a burden; it is a sacred and honorable duty. It is an acceptance that you alone are responsible for your preparation, your decisions, and your restraint. That responsibility doesn't end when the gun is holstered or the door is locked. It continues in how you interact with your community, how you teach your children, and how you model composure in an agitated world. Responsibility transforms defense from reaction to readiness, from impulse to intention.

Preparedness, at its best, is not a set of skills; it is a philosophy. It shapes how you think, how you move, how you love. It refines how you perceive danger, but more importantly, how you perceive peace. The loving defender is not defined by what they prepare to do, but by what they choose not to do. They carry great capability quietly. They train fiercely but live gently. They understand that restraint is the highest form of control. Their peace does not come from avoidance of conflict but from mastery of self.

To live this way is to live awake in a world that often prefers to sleep. It is to choose awareness over distraction, patience over pride, understanding over outrage. The defender's life is not glamorous; it's deliberate. It's built through thousands of small, unseen acts, the choice to walk away from provocation, to train when tired, to study the law when bored, to speak calmly when others shout. It's the accumulation of integrity over time.

Every act of preparation, every moment of reflection, every drop of sweat or second of study is part of the same painting, the portrait of a person who loves deeply enough to protect what matters most. And in that love, they find meaning. The loving defender doesn't train because they fear the world; they train because they value it. They don't carry a weapon because they crave dominance; they carry it because they understand responsibility. They don't walk in paranoia; they walk in peace earned through practice.

All the lessons of this book point to one truth: the goal has never been merely to survive; it has been to live rightly. To live as someone whose awareness doesn't harden into cynicism, whose strength doesn't twist into pride, whose readiness doesn't erode into fear. The ultimate preparation is balance, the harmony of vigilance and compassion, courage and humility, strength and empathy. That is the essence of the loving defender.

So this life, lived deliberately, isn't about waiting for the worst to happen. It's about moving through each day prepared to meet life fully, to respond wisely, to protect selflessly, to act justly, and to rest peacefully knowing you've done what you could. It's about building a life where readiness becomes second nature, where love and strength coexist without conflict, and where defense is not a reaction to danger but a reflection of devotion.

The loving defender's life is not an end goal; it's an ongoing practice. It evolves as you evolve. It asks you to keep learning, keep adjusting, keep refining. It invites you to see every day as another opportunity to strengthen your awareness, deepen your discipline, and expand your compassion. It's not about perfection. It's about pursuit; the steady quest for being ready for whatever may come, without losing sight of what makes life worth defending in the first place.

To live as a loving defender is to live awake, grateful, and grounded. It's to move through the world as both protector and peacemaker, aware that strength alone is not enough, and that peace without readiness is only an illusion. It's the balance between vigilance and grace, a quiet, steady way of living that honors both the fragility and the beauty of life.

Ultimately, that is what this entire journey will always be about, not merely surviving violence, but transcending fear. Not hardening the heart, but strengthening it. Not waiting for danger, but walking prepared, with love at the center of every choice. Afterall. Love, not anger, not pride, and not fear, is the most powerful reason to be ready.

That is the life worth living. That is the life prepared to prevail.

CONCLUSION

A LIFE PREPARED TO PREVAIL

When you've spent enough time learning about preparedness, awareness, and defense, it becomes clear that the goal was never just survival. It was understanding. The deeper you walk this path, the more you realize that readiness isn't about expecting the worst but about learning to live fully despite its possibility. It's about understanding what truly matters, and deciding, once and for all, that those things are worth protecting.

If you've made it this far, you already understand that this journey is not about weapons, tactics, or fear. It's about who you choose to be when life becomes uncertain. It's about building steadiness in a world that rewards distraction. It's about creating a life rooted in purpose, discipline, and quiet confidence, not because it makes you untouchable, but because it helps you meet each day with clarity.

Preparedness changes the way you see the world. It doesn't make you paranoid; it makes you present. You notice more the tone in someone's voice, the way a crowd moves, the weather shifting before a storm. You see fragility where others see routine, and opportunity where others see danger. Over time, this awareness evolves into something greater than just safety. It becomes appreciation. You stop taking peace for granted because you understand how quickly it can be lost, and that simple realization deepens every moment of calm, every ordinary day that passes without incident.

Living prepared means learning to hold two truths at once: that the world can be dangerous, and that it is still beautiful. You train for the first truth, but you live for the second. You strengthen your mind and body not because you expect to fight, but because you hope you never have to. You study, practice, and refine, not to control life, but to meet it with composure and love. Intention is what separates preparation from paranoia. The prepared person doesn't live against the world; they live responsibly within it.

There will be days when this mindset feels heavy, when the constant awareness and responsibility seem like too much to carry. That's natural. Preparation can sometimes feel isolating in a culture that prefers comfort to consciousness. However, always remember this: readiness isn't a burden, it's a gift. It allows you to move through life with fewer illusions and a deeper appreciation. It teaches you to see the weight of your choices, the reach of your influence, and the quiet power of restraint.

In the end, being prepared isn't about predicting what will happen; it's about deciding who you will be when it does. You can't control the future, but you can control your readiness for it. You can control your awareness, your habits, your integrity, and your peace. That control, the calm self-possession, is what gives life its steadiness, even when everything else is uncertain.

If this book has done its job, it hasn't filled you with fear; it's grounded you in perspective. It's reminded you that strength and kindness can coexist, that vigilance and compassion are not opposites, and that living prepared is really just another way of saying you've chosen to live intentionally. You've chosen to love deeply enough to protect what matters, to stay awake when it would be easier to drift, and to carry peace not as an accident, but as a duty.

So carry this mindset forward, not as doctrine, not as dogma, but as a quiet truth that shapes how you move through the world. Keep learning. Keep refining. Keep showing up for yourself and those who rely on you. Let your preparation evolve with your life, because both will continue to change.

Most importantly, live. Live fully, without apology. Laugh freely, love deeply, and rest without guilt. Readiness doesn't mean waiting for disaster; it means cherishing peace enough to defend it. It means knowing that you've done your part, and that whatever comes, you will meet it as someone who has already decided not to be a victim, not to be reckless, but to be deliberate.

That's what this journey has been leading toward from the very beginning, not the mechanics of defense, but the maturity of it. The loving defender's life is, at its heart, simply a life lived awake. It is the art of staying grounded in a chaotic world, calm in uncertainty, and compassionate in strength.

So go forward with confidence, not loud, not brash, but steady. Keep your awareness sharp, your heart humble, and your love fierce. The world will never be predictable, but you can be prepared. Moreover, that, more than anything else, is how you prevail.

www.ingramcontent.com/pod-product-compliance
Lightning Source LLC
LaVergne TN
LVHW020936090426
835512LV00020B/3380